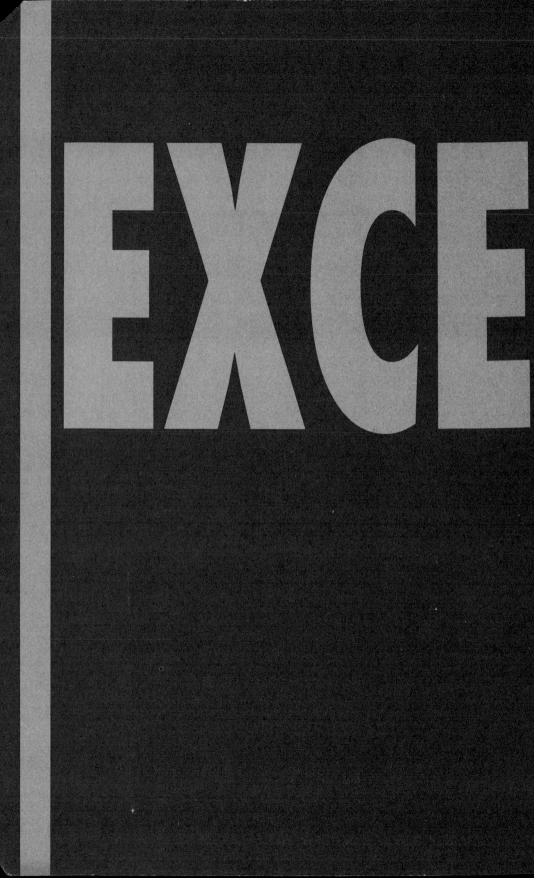

The Amazing Life of Stan Lee

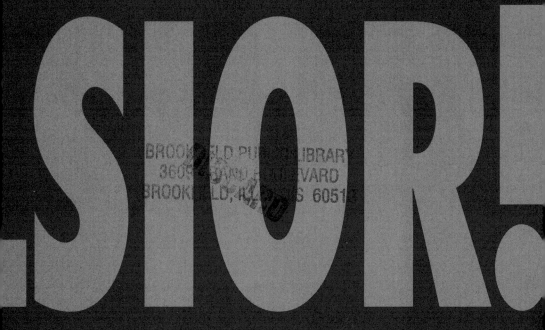

STAN LEE &

George Mair

A Fireside Book
Published by Simon & Schuster
New York   London   Toronto   Sydney   Singapore

FIRESIDE
Rockefeller Center
1230 Avenue of the Americas
New York, NY 10020

FIRESIDE and colophon are registered trademarks
of Simon & Schuster Inc.

For information regarding special discounts for bulk purchases,
please contact Simon & Schuster Special Sales at
1-800-456-6798 or business@simonandschuster.com

Designed by William P. Ruoto

Manufactured in the United States of America

1   3   5   7   9   10   8   6   4   2

Library of Congress Cataloging-in-Publication Data is available.

ISBN 0-684-87305-2

Contents

Stan's Soapbox

*H*ow did it happen?

How did I get into this? Me, a guy who's almost always written fantasy, suddenly having to deal with facts—the facts of my life.

Although, come to think of it, those facts themselves are pretty fantastic. If I hadn't lived the whole thing I might not even believe it. And, if you wanna talk about irony—!

During those strange, struggling, early years, I wallowed in embarrassment because I was a mere comicbook writer. And now, because of those same humble comicbooks, here I am the featured star of a real, grown-up book, the hero of my own life story.

There's probably a moral hidden there. Feel free to search for it as we roll along.

To tell the truth, I can't wait to read the pages that follow. Since so much of the past has managed to homogenize in the plot-cluttered recesses of my mind, it's a chance to rediscover little truths about my own inscrutable self and the titanically talented people I've worked with.

It'll also be a kick revisiting the weird and wonderful world of comics, a world inhabited by some of the most gifted artists and storytellers of our time, unsung geniuses who are only now beginning to receive the fame and respect that is so long overdue them.

In fact, as I write these hopefully imperishable words, virtually every major movie and TV studio is busily producing high-concept features based on, or inspired by, comicbook superheroes. Yep, our once-lowly costumed cavorters are now a mother lode of entertainment in today's quest for ever more thrills and excitement.

And so, thanks to Hollywood's burgeoning love affair with fantasy and special effects, I and the creations I've lived with lo these many years have suddenly become—way cool!

But first, a word about how this unorthodox book about my unorthodox life came to be.

My passionately persuasive literary agent, Susan Crawford, assured me that the entire reading public was panting for me to write my autobiography. (Yeah, right!) I told her I couldn't do it for two reasons. One, I'd never have time to do all the necessary research or to fine-tune a document chronicling seven long decades of memories, mirth, and misadventures. Two, I'd feel diffident about personally enumerating all my wonderful and endearing qualities; at the very least it could sound a mite immodest. Therefore, in one of the typical flashes of inspiration for which I'm so justly famous, I suggested that someone else simply write it as a biography, so the plaudits and accolades would not be attributed to my own unassuming self.

But Susan, with bulldog tenacity belying her cherubic features, said that my old friends at Simon & Schuster wanted it to have the flavor of my own style of writing (masochists that they were) and not some biographer's. Finally, when it seemed we were at an impasse, that most erudite editor, magisterial Matt Walker, got into the act. With the wisdom of Solomon—and the persistence of a piranha—he suggested it be a new type of biography, a "bio-autography," if you will. He and Susan twisted the arm of George Mair, biographer par excellence and all around swell guy, to collaborate on the book with me. George would diligently do the research, organize the factual material, and write the flattering portions of the book (which I hoped would be the major part, of course), while I would kibitz throughout the tome by adding items of philosophical profundity and inane inconsequence whenever you least expect it.

So what you now behold with breathless anticipation is the world's first bio-autography. Hell, you wouldn't expect anything less from me, would you?

Okay, now that that's out of the way, I'd better start wrapping this up so that George can do his thing. And what better way to do that than by telling you these seventy-plus years have been a wild and wondrous ride for me. I want you to have as much fun reading about them as I had living them. In fact, it'll be even easier for you. You can share all the funky, frivolous, far-out foibles without having to write a page of dialogue or draw a single picture yourself.

But, before I turn you loose so you can get to the good stuff, here are a couple of sentences I wrote some years ago to describe my feelings about what Marvel Comics represents. The entire passage is actually longer than this, but I fear if I give you the whole thing, there won't be a dry eye left in the place.

Marvel is a cornucopia of fantasy, a wild idea, a swashbuckling attitude, an escape from the humdrum and prosaic. It's a serendipitous feast for the mind, the eye, and the imagination, a literate celebration of unbridled creativity, coupled with a touch of rebellion and an insolent desire to spit in the eye of the dragon.

There you have it, my take on Marvel and the fantasy genre in general, and perhaps my own philosophy in particular. If those words strike a chord with you, read on. If they don't, I'd rather not know.

So let's not waste another minute. My whole life is on the pages ahead, awaiting your validation. I hope you don't mind company while you read, 'cause I'll be right there with you all the way.

Excelsior!

The Start of Something Big

It may have seemed ordinary to some, but it was an event that would affect the minds and lives of millions in the years to come.

Stanley Martin Lieber was born on December 28, 1922, on Ninety-eighth Street and West End Avenue in New York City, the first child of Jack and Celia Lieber, both Romanian immigrants among thousands of others who came to America, became American citizens, and settled in New York. For Stan's family and millions of others, the 1920s and the Great Depression were a struggle to survive. Jack Lieber was trained as a dress cutter and worked in New York's garment district sporadically until the Depression hit in 1929. After that, he was frustrated by his inability to find steady work, no matter how hard he tried. At one point, he invested his meager savings in a small diner, but that soon failed. Still, no matter how bleak things became, Stan's mother, Celia, never stopped dreaming that her son would somehow, someday become a great success.

I always felt sorry for my father. He was a good man, honest and caring. He wanted the best for his family, as most parents do. But the times were against him. At the height of the Depression there were just no jobs to be had.

Seeing the demoralizing effect that his unemployment had on his spirit, making him feel that he just wasn't needed, gave me a

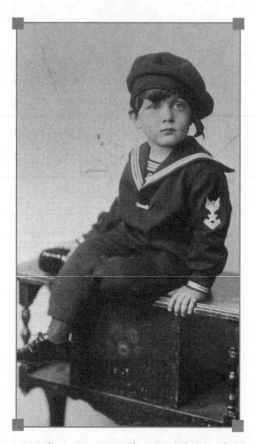

Chapter 1

Some sailor! I got seasick even taking a bath.

feeling I've never been able to shake. It's a feeling that the most important thing for a man is to have work to do, to be busy, to be needed. Today, I never feel more fulfilled than when I'm working on a number of projects at once, which is really nuts because I'm always wishing I had more free time. Still, when I'm busy I feel needed, and that makes me feel good.

There you have it, instant psychiatry, and it didn't cost either of us a cent.

I always wished my mother and father would lavish as much

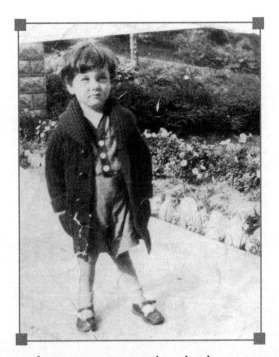

The Age of Innocence. No superhero battles to worry about.

love on each other as they did on my younger brother, Larry, and me. They were both good, loving parents, and I think the only thing that gave them any pleasure was their children. My brother and I always regretted that fate had not been kinder to them and that they couldn't have had happier lives. They must have loved each other when they married, but my earliest recollections were of the two of them arguing, quarreling incessantly. Almost always it was over money, or the lack of it. I realized at an early age how the specter of poverty, the never-ending worry about not having enough money to buy groceries or to pay the rent, can cast a cloud over a marriage. I'll always regret the fact that, by the time I was earning enough money to make things easier for them, it was too late.

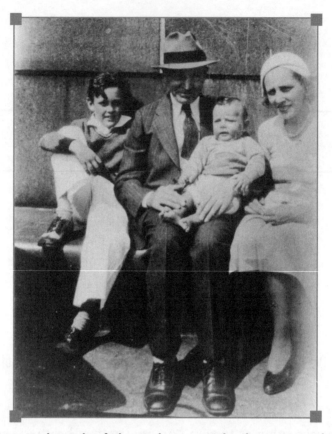

My mother Celia, father Jack, younger brother Larry, and
Mr. Casual in his new white ducks.

My mother spent almost all her time cleaning our small apartment or cooking in the kitchen. As for my father, I used to see that
poor guy, day after day, sitting at a little table in our small living room
reading the want ads. He wasn't able to phone for an appointment
for interviews because we didn't have a phone, so he'd go out every
morning and return hours later with the same dejected expression
on his face. Thinking of him reading the want ads, walking the
streets, sitting at that little table staring into space, I can imagine the
depression he felt. Forced idleness is a terrible thing.

Even in those difficult times there was one joyful thing for Stan. It was the thing that eventually changed his life forever. It was his love for reading, for losing himself in the magical world of books.

I can't remember when I first learned to read, nor can I remember a time when I wasn't reading. It was my escape from the dreariness and sadness of my home life. I read everything I could find, everywhere, every chance I got. In school, reading and composition were always my best subjects. At every meal at home—breakfast, lunch, or dinner—I'd have a book or magazine to read while I ate. One of the first presents my mother bought me was a little stand to keep on the kitchen table to rest a book against while eating. I remember it had little clips on the bottom to hold the pages in place. I treasured that little stand for years. My mother used to say that if there was nothing to read, I'd read the labels on ketchup bottles, which I did. Actually, I preferred *The Hardy Boys* to ketchup bottles, even though ketchup-bottle labels were easier. In truth, one of my darkest secrets is that I've never been comfortable eating unless I'm also reading. One of my greatest childhood pleasures was to sit with my legs over the arm of an upholstered chair reading while I snacked on buttered crusts of rye bread.

The great stock market crash came when Stan was seven. While he didn't understand high finance at that age, he did sense the hard times everybody was enduring. For Stan and millions of others, the books and the movies they saw over and over again offered relief. Such entertainments helped transport them into the world of mystery, adventure, and excitement. This was a world into which Stan moved as a youth and, in some ways, one from which he has never returned. Stan recalls how he began creating his first stories.

Unable to afford West End Avenue any longer, we moved to a tiny rear apartment in upper Manhattan's Washington Heights. Besides my reading, I began scribbling little illustrated stories to amuse myself. I would draw a straight horizontal line for the horizon and then add stick figures above it, around which I built simple stories and plot lines. I was, without knowing it, creating my first comicbooks. This was a make-believe world I loved because I could retreat to it from the outside—particularly from school.

In school, I was always something of an outsider. That's because I was usually the youngest kid in my class and in my social group. This was part of the impact the Depression had on families like mine. My mother wanted me to finish school as soon as possible so I could get a job and help support the family, which is another reason I had the work ethic drummed into me at an early age. I studied hard and skipped grades, which put me in with older kids. But as you might imagine, it's no fun being the youngest kid in the class.

During that time, the adult who had the most impact on me was my favorite teacher, Leon B. Ginsberg Jr. (It's amazing how I still remember his name.) He would entertain the class with humorous and exciting stories to illustrate teaching points. It was Mr. Ginsberg who first made me realize that learning could be fun, that it was easier to reach people, to hold their attention, to get points across, with humor than any other way. It was a lesson I never forgot, a lesson I've tried to apply to everything I do.

Besides Mr. Ginsberg, one other thing made a tremendous impression on me. It wasn't a person. It was a bicycle, my first two-wheeler. When I rode it, in my imagination I was a mighty knight atop a noble steed. That bike was my best friend because it gave me a feeling of freedom. So what if our family didn't have a car. I finally had wheels. I could ride all over the city, go wherever I pleased. No kid ever loved a bike more than I loved mine.

Apart from the joys of riding my bike and reading books, there were phases of life that I still recall as very depressing. Though it may seem like a trivial thing, I was saddened by the fact that my family always lived in a rear apartment—never one facing

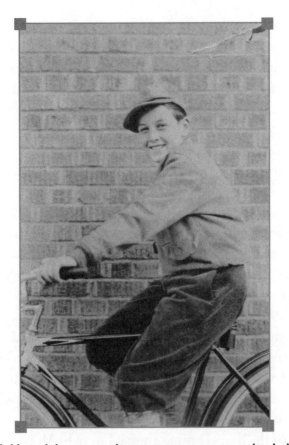

It might look like a bike to you, but to me it was a two-wheeled space ship.

the street. Looking out the window, all we could see was the brick wall of the building across the alley. I could never look and see if the other kids were out in the street playing stickball or doing anything that I might join in.

Today, my home is on a hilltop in Los Angeles, where we have a view stretching from the Pacific Ocean to downtown. After all these years, I finally feel I can look outside and see what's going on.

A real depressing time for me was summer, when most of the kids went away to camps with unpronounceable Indian names.

What made this depressing for me—aside from not being able to send postcards home from places like Camp UgaUgaTa and Camp Monga-Wonga-Donga, or whatever—was that I was usually alone in the city. Most of my friends would be at camp and I'd be hanging around the school yard, hoping someone would come by for a game of handball.

But it wasn't all bad. I always had my reading.

Of course, I read comicbooks, too, but they were different than the kind today. They were mostly reprints of newspaper strips: *The Katzenjammer Kids, Skippy, Dick Tracy, Smitty,* and *The Gumps.* I loved them. But then, I loved almost anything written on the printed page. The first "real" comicbook that impressed me was *Captain America,* done by Joe Simon and Jack Kirby, which was later on.

My mother, bless her, always encouraged my reading, not that I required much prodding. In fact, she often asked me to read aloud to her, and being the ham that I am, I enjoyed doing that, imagining I was on some Broadway stage reading for a vast, entranced audience. It's funny, but I always seem to feel, whatever I'm doing, that I'm doing it for the wildly appreciative human race.

Some of the books I most enjoyed were by H. G. Wells, Arthur Conan Doyle, Mark Twain, and Edgar Rice Burroughs. Then there were the seemingly limitless tales of the Hardy Boys, Don Sturdy, Tom Swift, the Boy Allies, and so many other series of mystery and adventure which sold in hardcover editions for the whopping price of fifty cents, and which I suspected were all written by the same prolific genius under a dozen different pseudonyms.

After a while, my tastes in reading became more eclectic. I discovered Edgar Allan Poe, Charles Dickens, Edmond Rostand, Omar Khayyám, Émile Zola, and, of course, Shakespeare. While I'm sure most of the Bard's work was way over my then juvenile head, I was fascinated by the rhythm of his words, by the flowery language, the "What ho, Horatio!" type of outpourings. The same with the Bible. Though I'm not particularly religious, I love that style of writing, the almost poetical phrasing and the "thees" and "thous" and "begats," which can make the simplest thought seem fraught with drama. I suspect that both Shakespeare and the Bible had a considerable effect on my writing in later years when I did comics about Norse gods, incantation-spouting magicians, and long-winded philosophers from outer space.

And then there were the movies. For me, going to a movie was one of the greatest events imaginable. There on the screen were worlds that dazzled my mind, worlds of magic and wonder, worlds which I longed to inhabit, if only in imagination. In upper Manhattan, on 181st Street, there were five theaters within three blocks. The area was heaven to me. I could see Errol Flynn, Charlie Chan, Roy Rogers, Sherlock Holmes, Gunga Din, Frankenstein, Moby Dick, Charlie Chaplin, and King Kong. Even now, I feel a twinge of excitement just thinking about all that wonderment.

Stan was the only child in the household for nine years until his brother, Larry, was born. Later, Larry would talk about how it was growing up in the family: "I remember, in terms of Stan and myself, my mother always spoke so highly of Stan. At the time, I used to play a lot and run around and she'd say to me, 'Why don't you read books the way your brother does and be literate like Stan?' And I had this feeling that Stan was wonderful. She told me once that, when Stan was a child, one of the schoolteachers said, 'He reminds me of President Roosevelt.' That's a helluva thing—my older brother was President Roosevelt! I didn't really know him, so I think I built up a kinda hero worship there."

I always regretted that I was nine years older than Larry because it was a little tough for us to play together. He's a great guy, but in those days I didn't get to know him as well as I would have wanted to. When he was five, I was fourteen. It's not too easy for a teenager to hang around with a five-year-old. And when he was old enough for me to pal around with, I was off to the army. But he's a terrific person and the fact that we weren't very close in those early years is my loss.

One high point in Stan's young life around this time involved a corre-spondent for the Chicago Tribune *whose daring adventures en-tranced the country and were more like something Stan would know from movies than from real life. His name was Floyd Gibbons and his first big adventure was to chase after the Mexican renegade Pancho Villa, who had raided across the American border and threatened to kill any American he caught in Mexico. Villa's incursion so infuriated President Woodrow Wilson that he dispatched an army under Gen-eral Jack Pershing into Mexico to capture the bandit—all to no avail. Gibbons, however, found Villa and rode with him through three major battles while writing dispatches for the American press. Several years later, America was in World War I and Gibbons survived being sunk at sea while en route to Europe on the ship* Laconia. *Almost fa-tally wounded at the assault on Belleau Wood, Gibbons lost an eye, but he returned a hero and wrote a newspaper column that Stan read avidly. At the age of ten, Stan so admired Gibbons that he sent him a fan letter and actually got an answer, a response that he saved for years. Stan couldn't get over the fact that the world-famous Floyd Gibbons had actually taken the time to write him a letter. It might have been that experience that impressed upon Stan the importance of communicating with one's fans, but that's a story yet to come.*

Eventually, Stan got so caught up in what he was reading that he decided to try his hand at writing, too. When he was fifteen, the Herald-Tribune, *one of New York's biggest newspapers at that time, had a continuing contest for high school students called "The Biggest News of the Week Contest." Those who entered were to write, as pro-fessionally as possible, in five hundred words or less, what they con-sidered to be the most important news story of the week. Stan entered the contest three times and won first prize three weeks in a row. The editor finally sent him a letter asking him to stop submitting and give someone else a chance.*

I don't remember the editor's name, but his suggestion probably changed my life. He advised me to think about becoming a professional writer. I did think about it. In fact, I've never stopped thinking about it.

Of course, writing and bike riding weren't the only things in my life. As time went by and my voice deepened, my libido began to kick in. I was eventually initiated into the mysteries and pleasures of sex.

Today, one of my great regrets is that I cannot remember the name of the daughter of the neighborhood candy store proprietor with whom I lost my virginity. It's not that I didn't enjoy it or that I wasn't grateful for the enchanting episode. It's just that she'll always remain a mystery woman from my past life, like the little red-headed girl in the *Peanuts* comic strip whose memory has always haunted Charlie Brown. And if she's reading this now, here's a personal message to her: Please don't be embarrassed. I'm referring to the daughter of a different candy store owner.

Working was always an imperative in the Lieber household. As soon as Stan could, in his spare time after his high school classes, he began a series of part-time jobs, including writing obituary notices for a news service. When a celebrity died, the next edition of the paper carried a write-up of his life, much of which was already in the files except for the time, cause, and place of death. Even though the work paid well, Stan eventually gave it up. He found it too depressing to be writing about people in the past tense.

That led to a job writing publicity for the National Tuberculosis Hospital in Denver. He liked the work but was never quite clear about what he was supposed to be publicizing. (Was he to convince people to get tuberculosis so they could go to this hospital?) He also delivered sandwiches from the Jack May drugstore to offices in Rockefeller Center. Most deliveries rated a dime tip, and the more deliveries he made, the more tips he'd receive. Stan still proudly remembers that he ran faster than any of the other delivery boys. Some days he made more than two dollars in tips, which he claims was something of a record for that period.

One job that was a blast was being an usher at the Rivoli Theater on Broadway, a few blocks north of Times Square. In those days, being an usher in a Broadway movie house was a big deal. You wore a Gilbert-and-Sullivan type uniform and were expected to conduct yourself like a West Pointer. The Rivoli had four aisles, with an usher stationed at the head of each one. I remember once I wanted to tell something to the usher at the next aisle, so I discreetly snapped my fingers to get his attention. Bad move! The manager came storming over and glared at me. He told me that ushers never snap their fingers. Ushers could only jiggle their flashlights. Only the manager snapped his fingers. I was learning about executive perks at an early age. It's lucky I wasn't court-martialed.

But I did have one unforgettable experience on my own little aisle one day. Eleanor Roosevelt came in, accompanied by a horde of Secret Service men. Out of the four available aisles, mine was the one she chose. I couldn't believe it. I was about to show the First Lady of the United States of America to her seat. So, with my shoulders back, my chest out, my head held high, and my trusty flashlight shining its beam on the floor in front of her, I proudly walked down the aisle, stiff as a ramrod, and promptly tripped over the foot of some moron who had his leg stretched out in the aisle. Next thing I knew, Mrs. Franklin Delano Roosevelt, that sainted woman, had her hands on my shoulders, trying to help me to my feet as she whispered solicitously, "Are you all right, young man?" It wasn't my proudest moment.

At DeWitt Clinton High School in the Bronx there was a fella I admired very much. I didn't know him well but he was one of my first heroes. His name was John J. McKenna Jr., and he was a grade or two above me. No, he wasn't a football quarterback or a jock of any sort. He simply sold subscriptions to the *New York Times.* He'd go into a classroom, tell the teacher what he was offering, and ask if he could address the class. The teachers always agreed because they were glad to have him encourage their students to subscribe to a paper like the *Times.*

I remember the day he came into my class.

"Hello, I'm John J. McKenna Junior, and I'm here to offer you a subscription to the *Times.* Here is why you should read it . . ."

I was one of the first to subscribe, but the main thing on my mind was, Man, if only I could address an audience as confidently as that and speak off the cuff as glibly as he. He spoke for about ten full minutes, looking his audience straight in the eye, never once fumbling or losing the attention of the class. I was terribly impressed by the smooth, easygoing way he made his pitch and the way he managed to hold the interest of the students while talking about a subject that normally would bore the pants off them.

I decided that I wanted to be able to speak that way, to be able to hold the attention of an audience the way he did. Now here's the odd part. If this were a work of fiction, I'd be telling you how McKenna and I became lifelong friends. But, in truth, I don't believe we ever met. I doubt that he was even aware of me—and it mystifies me how I, who have the world's worst memory, have never forgotten his name.

He never knew it, but McKenna, with his great gift of gab, who could make a tough teenage audience listen attentively to every word he had to say, was one of my first role models (after the aforementioned Leon B. Ginsberg Jr., of course).

A year later, in one of life's little triumphs, when I became a senior at Clinton High, I ended up doing exactly what he did. I too made speeches selling subscriptions in classes, except I represented the *Herald-Tribune*. I was always proud of the fact that I managed to follow in McKenna's footsteps—and the fact that I thought I did as well as he did. Hey, maybe even better.

The government under President Franklin D. Roosevelt had created the Works Progress Administration (WPA) to give unemployed people some work and keep them off the streets. Stan was a beneficiary of this government program but probably not in exactly the way that President Roosevelt had in mind. Some time after graduating from high school, Stan went to a stage show at a local Y and got a crush on one of the girls onstage that night. He decided that the easiest way to meet her was to join the WPA Federal Theatre Project (FTP) himself. He did, and the two had a romantic attachment for quite a while. Yet the WPA theater had its other attractions.

After appearing in a few shows, I said, "Hey, this is for me." I had gotten the acting bug. And I wasn't the only one. Orson Welles was in it, too. Yes, *the* Orson Welles. I must confess I never actually palled around with him, because he was at another WPA theater in another part of the city, but hey, we literally were both in the WPA together, so I used to tell people, "Oh, yeah, Orson and I appeared in shows for the WPA." If my listeners thought we had been costars, who was I to disillusion them? In fact, years later when I lectured at various colleges, I'd often mention that little story and add the fact that I hoped Orson Welles was likewise lecturing somewhere and saying, "I used to act in the WPA Federal Theatre Project—with Stan Lee." But just between us, that would have been most unlikely.

Ever since those fun days, I've always thought it would be great to make a career of acting, mainly because it's easier than working, that is if you can tolerate the boredom when you're not actually performing. But in those days, it had to be a driving passion with you because the WPA paid next to nothing, and I had a couple of parents to support. So I had to give it up. And besides, after a while my romance had cooled with that certain girl.

I also wanted to be a lawyer. I had seen a movie starring Warren William called *The Mouthpiece.* There was an unforgettable courtroom scene where William, playing a famous trial lawyer, absolutely hypnotized the jury—and me—with his theatrics and impassioned oratory. It never occurred to me that legal work consisted mainly of studying documents and spending hours preparing briefs—to me, it was just performing in a courtroom, just like being an actor. So I daydreamed that it would be great to be a lawyer as well as an actor. It seemed so dramatic, so theatrical. If only it wasn't necessary to go to law school.

Oh, there was one other thing, too. I was a total fanatic about advertising. I'd have loved to have made a career of creating ad campaigns. Even today, when I read a newspaper or magazine, I'll spend as much time reading the ads as the rest of the mag. Same with TV. I enjoy the commercials more than many of the shows themselves. I love looking at ads and thinking, I would have written it this way, or Wow! That's even better than I could have thought up. Of course, that thought doesn't hit me too often.

I used to love the old Volkswagen ads of years ago when they admitted that the "beetle" was funny looking, and they succeeded in making a plus of that by injecting humor and empathy. Years later I tried to use that same psychology at Marvel Comics. But more about that later.

Now that I think of it, I suppose what I've really enjoyed most all of my life was relating to the public in some way or other. In fact, I just remembered something else. I'm also a big fan of magic. In high school, I wasn't too good at card tricks or coin tricks, but for some reason or other I was a whiz at thimble tricks. You see, on the edge of most thimbles are little lips, which make them easy to manipulate. I became adept at doing sleight of hand with thimbles, and occasionally gave demonstrations at our school's Magic Club, where I called myself "Thimbilini" while fantasizing that I was performing on a big Broadway stage before an audience of thousands. Yep, that was me, never far from a private fantasy world of my own.

One job Stan had that he didn't like at all was as an office boy for a major trouser manufacturer. He was located on a floor filled with dozens of trouser salesmen, each in his own little cubicle. Stan was one of a pair of office boys and whenever anybody in the shop wanted something, he'd holler, "Boy!" Whichever office boy was closest was supposed to drop whatever he was doing and come running. Just as he had when delivering sandwiches in Rockefeller Center, Stan ran the fastest and did the most fetching. But no one seemed to notice or to care. The thing that galled Stan the most was the fact that no one ever took the trouble to learn his name. He didn't want to go through life being known as "boy." His experience in that office of over one hundred people sparked his concern in later years with trying to show respect for others and giving even the lowest-level employee a sense of dignity.

Stan's entire experience in that shop was something of a nightmare to him. The manufacturer had "cutting tickets" that listed the shapes, materials, and prices of different kinds of trousers. Those so-called cutting tickets consisted of very heavy sheets of paper, like flexible cardboard, about four feet long and a foot-and-a-half high. It was Stan's responsibility to file them sequentially in big, coffin-like bins. There was always a shortage of bins, so Stan inevitably had to squeeze more tickets into fewer bins than there was room for. He came home every night with his cuticles cut and bloody from trying to force those long, flexible sheets between all the other tightly packed sheets. To make matters worse, two days before Christmas the company decided to fire one of the office boys. The other boy had been hired a month before Stan, so on the basis of seniority it was Stan who got the boot, notwithstanding the fact that he worked twice as hard as the boy whom the company was retaining. In one of the few vengeful acts of his life, Stan got so angry about the way they dismissed him that when he left, he took a few of those tightly packed cutting-ticket containers and turned them upside down, scattering the tickets all over the room. Now, many decades later, he wonders if those salesmen are still trying to put them back in order. He hopes so.

However, leaving that job didn't mean I could spend time loafing. I needed to work. When I graduated from DeWitt Clinton High in 1939 at age seventeen, the immediate order of business was to shift from a temporary job to a permanent one. My uncle, Robbie Solomon, told me they might be able to use someone at a publishing company where he worked. The idea of being involved in publishing definitely appealed to me. Unlike the trouser business, it would be an opportunity to relate to the public. So I contacted the man Robbie said did the hiring, Joe Simon, and applied for a job. He took me on and I began working as a gofer for eight dollars a week at this small company located in the McGraw-Hill Building on Forty-second Street at Ninth Avenue, on the west side of Manhattan.

I didn't realize it at the time, but I had embarked on my life's career.

Editor by Default

Careerwise, one of the most important people in Stan's life was Martin Goodman, a somewhat distant relative. They had not been particularly close before Stan got into the world of comicbooks, but as time went by that was to change.

The publishing company my uncle Robbie worked for was owned by Martin Goodman, who was married to my cousin Jean. Martin and I had never had much to do with each other before I started working at his company. We had almost nothing in common since I was much younger than he and fresh out of high school, while he, although comparatively young himself, was already a successful publisher with a growing business. Even after I joined the company I had very little to do with him in the beginning. To him, I was just that young cousin of his wife's, and he probably hoped they'd find something for me to do where I wouldn't screw things up too much. I hoped so, too.

While Stan was growing up during the 1920s and 1930s, Martin Goodman was building an enterprise around which Stan's future would ultimately revolve.

Goodman was one of the earliest publishers in the field of pulp magazines. These provided inexpensive entertainment for the masses who could not afford to buy pricey clothbound books. Some of the pulp titles Goodman published in the late 1930s were forerunners of the coming comicbook trend: Star Detective, Uncanny Stories, Complete Western Book, *and* Mystery Tales. *As with all good businessmen, Martin was always on the lookout for new products, while tracking what his competition was doing. This became particularly urgent when movies and comicbooks, which were cheaper to enjoy, began to encroach on the sales of his pulp magazines. Unable to beat the competition, Martin decided to join the trend and begin publishing comics.*

Others were also getting into the comicbook field, including a company named Funnies, Inc. Alas, the Funnies people not only had insufficient money to operate, but they faced stiff competition from National Periodicals and All-American Comics (who would later merge and become DC Comics). That's when a Funnies salesman, Frank Torpey, approached Martin Goodman and offered to sell some of the Funnies superhero features to Goodman's own company. This deal launched Martin Goodman into superhero comicbooks in a big way starting in October 1939 with Marvel Comics #1, *which the* Overstreet Comic Book Price Guide *calls "possibly the most sought-after comic of the Golden Age."*

The comicbook form of narrative storytelling was growing stunningly fast. The number of different titles, heroes, heroines, and adventures multiplied as quickly as their creators' imaginations permitted. The stock-in-trade for the heroes of those stories included a cape, tights, mask, and secret powers and identities. One historian said, "Comics became million-copy sellers because theirs was a world with no seam between reality and magic. It was a world of super-acrobatics and ultra-pratfalls where common clay became uncommon heroes."

Before Stan was hired, Timely (which was the name under which Goodman published his comicbooks) had some brilliant free-lance artists, one of whom, Bill Everett, invented the Sub-Mariner.

Another of Timely's legendary freelancers, Carl Burgos, invented an android, the Human Torch—a being created artificially in a laboratory, as was Frankenstein's monster. Burgos and Everett were both multifaceted talents, doing all the writing, artwork, and lettering themselves. The Human Torch was not a typical superhero devoted to doing good for the world, as was Superman. Instead, he was a mixed-up, unstable being trapped in a scientifically created body—a pattern for many superheroes to follow. As for the Sub-Mariner, he hated the whole human race and often costarred in the same comicbook as the Human Torch in epic tales where they fought to the death—except Marvel heroes never died. Both characters appeared in Goodman's most successful comicbook at that time, Marvel Comics.*

Goodman was lucky with those characters. Business was getting good enough for him to hire his own full-time creative staff to supplement what he was getting from freelancers. That's when he took the plunge and hired his first regular creative staff person, Joe Simon, a twenty-four-year-old combination editor, artist, and writer, who would later officially hire Stan. Goodman wanted Simon to develop additional new comicbook titles to capitalize on the lucrative trade. Simon created* Daring Mystery Comics *and* Mystic Comics, *which were weak because their characters (the Phantom Reporter, Rudy the Robot, the Fin, the Blue Blaze, Master Mind, Excello, and Flexo the Rubber Man) were ultimately neither strong nor commanding. When none of these caught on, Goodman hired another artist to help, Jacob Kurtzberg, who would go through four name changes before ending up Jack Kirby. Together, Joe Simon and Jack Kirby created* Red Raven Comics, *which appeared once in August 1940 before Goodman canceled it for reasons that remain obscure. It was with* Captain America *that they later really hit their stride.*

The public reaction to Marvel Comics #1 *was very positive, convincing Goodman that comics were a type of publishing worth pursuing. But another body was needed to help with the grunt work, to proofread, handle the mail, and run whatever errands were neces-*

sary. That's when a young man by the name of Stanley Lieber arrived at his door, ready to begin working as a general gofer.

My first day on the job at Timely, Martin Goodman seemed surprised to see me. He sounded puzzled as he asked me, "What are you doing here?" I didn't know if Robbie had neglected to mention that I had been interviewed and accepted by editor Joe Simon, or if Simon himself had forgotten to tell him, or maybe it was Martin's way of kidding. I never did find out and I was kept too busy to worry about it after that.

Although Martin only asked me that question once, I would ask myself that same question a thousand times over the years that followed.

As bosses go, Martin was pretty much okay. He was somewhat aloof in the beginning, but why not—we weren't exactly drinking buddies. Timely was a fairly small company and most of the staff called him by his first name. One thing about him was obvious— he enjoyed being a boss. He took lots of time off to play golf, would nap on his office couch almost every afternoon, and, in later years, enjoyed playing Scrabble with anyone in the company who had the time. Alas, that was never me. But he still managed to keep an eye on things and he knew the publishing business inside and out. A self-educated man, he was sharp as a tack and nobody knew the intricacies of magazine circulation better than he. If he had been more ambitious, I think his company could have become one of the giants in publishing, but Martin seemed quite satisfied just to make a good living and not have to work too hard. It frustrated me, because I always wished we could have done more and gone farther. But I kept those thoughts to myself. In those days I considered myself lucky to have a job, and an interesting job at that.

There were only a handful of people in the comics department when I started there. Joe Simon was the editor and Jack Kirby was the staff artist. Some artwork was bought from outside sources, but Jack seemed to carry most of the load. He and Joe also did most of the scriptwriting themselves.

Then my big break happened. As the number of comics expanded, there was more work than Joe and Jack could handle and, since I knew the difference between a declarative sentence and a baseball bat, I was given a chance to write some things myself. My very first comicbook work—are you paying attention, Smithsonian?—was a two-page text piece entitled "The Traitor's Revenge!" Those two-page text pieces had to be included among the illustrated panels in order to qualify for the post office's cheap magazine rate. Nobody ever took the time to read them, but I didn't care. I had become a published author. I was a pro!

My story appeared in *Captain America* #3, which was dated May 1941. My first actual comicbook script, what was called a "filler," came two issues later in *Captain America* #5 dated August 1941, as I proudly penned a story with the ultra-sophisticated title of "Headline Hunter, Foreign Correspondent." I was barely out of high school and I was now a full-fledged comicbook writer, which is far better than being partially fledged.

Good ol' Timely published a variety of comicbook themes, from Westerns to crime to horror to superheroes, and I loved being connected with them all, but by then I had decided that nothing would stop me from one day writing the Great American Novel. Typical, isn't it? A guy gets a few comicbook scripts under his belt and decides he's the next Hemingway. Being only seventeen at the time and not yet having become the incredibly sophisticated and knowledgeable superperson that I am today, I somehow felt it would not be seemly to take my name, which was certain to one day win a Pulitzer, and sign it to mere, humble comic strips. Thus, I was caught up in the fantasy of using a pen name, something suitable for strips, while saving my real name for the saga that would make me immortal. And that's how Stan Lee was born. I simply cut my first name in half and slyly changed the *y* to a second *e*.

Later, when I was writing a whole mess of stories in every issue, Martin decided it shouldn't look as if Timely could only afford one writer, so I adopted additional pen names. At various times I was S.T. Anley, Stan Martin, Neel Nats (guess what that spells backwards!), and others that I've since forgotten. All of that was to save my real name, Stanley Martin Lieber, for the prize-winning novel I would one day write.

The ironic part is, I recently wrote a novel, *The Alien Factor,* together with a talented collaborator named Stan Timmons. The only name my publisher would let me use was Stan Lee, because he said that's the one the public knows. It's like something out of O. Henry, right?

As for my nom de plume, in time my wife, Joanie, and I had a lot of trouble with car licenses, passports, and charge accounts because our last name was legally Lieber but everybody knew us as Lee. So, Joanie and I finally took the plunge and changed it to Lee in order to simplify our lives. Today, I am legally and officially Stan Lee, but I have been giving some thought to changing it back to Lieber—just to confuse everybody.

Now, for the accountants among you who care about such things, back in the early days of comics, artists and writers were paid on a piecework basis, that is, so much per page. Most are still paid that way today, but the present rates bear no resemblance to the old ones. I think I received about fifty cents a page for the first script I wrote back in the forties. The more pages you could grind out, the more money you made. It was like when I delivered sandwiches for the Jack May drugstore and got a tip for each delivery. The faster I ran, the more money I made, and at Timely it was the same thing. The faster I wrote, the more pages I turned out and the more half-dollars I made. So the comicbook writer had to be a dedicated comicbook freak—he certainly couldn't be in it for the money. And, unlike other forms of writing, there were no royalty payments at the end of the road. No residuals. No copyright ownership. You wrote your pages, got your check, and that was it.

I worked with Joe Simon and Jack Kirby for a relatively short time at Timely, but long enough to realize that the partnership of those two is one of the great not-fully-told stories of the comic-book industry. While I can't tell their complete story here, let me just share a few things about them. Jack was a native New Yorker, as I was, and about six years older than I. He started drawing professionally in 1935, doing such unlikely projects as *Betty Boop* and *Popeye*, along with some forgotten newspaper strips such as *Black Buccaneer, Socko the Seadog,* and *Abdul Jones.* He teamed up with Joe Simon at Timely in 1941 and that's when his talent began to blossom, particularly with *Captain America,* which is arguably their greatest creation. Jack and Joe later drifted around to various companies over the coming years, ultimately splitting up in 1956, with Jack coming back in 1959 to work with me again at what was about to become Marvel Comics, and where we did some of our greatest superheroes—*The Fantastic Four, The X-Men, The Silver Surfer.* But I'm getting ahead of myself.

Joe Simon was born in upstate New York and got into comics doing a strip called Blue Beetle *before he linked up with Jack. As with all artistic teams, outsiders used to speculate over who did what in the team, but whatever way it worked out, those two were something special in the history of comicbooks.*

Simon and Kirby worked well together in producing Captain America *without ego problems interfering with their tight production schedule. A new system of turning out comics was growing in the industry, with writing, art, and lettering each done separately. With Simon and Kirby, it didn't matter; each of them could do just about anything. They worked at breakneck speed to meet the demand for more and more* Captain America *stories. Their main goal was to make more money for everybody (including themselves, as they owned a piece of* Captain America*) and not worry about credit or personal egos.*

Working for Simon and Kirby was an education for me. I admired their talents and their professionalism, so it was like working for two idols. Visually, they would have made a perfect comedy team inasmuch as Joe was very tall and thin while Jack was shorter and stocky. We never became very friendly at that time because they never thought of me as a peer, and there's no reason why they should have. I had started as an inexperienced apprentice, and it's hard to live that first impression down. Anyway, I didn't work with them long enough for our relationship to change significantly—or for them to learn the sheer wonderfulness of me.

Thinking back sixty years, I believe the way the two of them worked in the beginning is that Joe was technically the writer and editor and Jack the artist, although I'm sure that Jack had great input in the stories. Sort of like it would be later on when Jack and I worked together on the superheroes we created. What I do remember is that, most of the time, Jack was sitting at his drawing board working on the artwork, chewing on his cigar, and mumbling to himself, or maybe he was muttering, or it might have been humming. Due to the heavy clouds of cigar smoke, I could never get close enough to find out. Joe was a partial mirror of Jack in that he also incessantly had a cigar in his mouth, but in his case I could tell the difference between his muttering, mumbling, and humming as he paced the office. Unfortunately, my initial experience with the two of them was relatively short-lived because they quit Timely a few months after I started working there. And no, it wasn't because of me!

Simon and Kirby had been under enormous pressure. Not only did Goodman want them to keep turning out stories, but he also wanted them to continue developing new material. They did this in All Winners Comics, *which featured Captain America, the Human Torch, the Sub-Mariner, the Destroyer, and the fastest hero in the world, the Whizzer. Goodman was thrilled at how well those books sold, but his* *two stars were working very hard—harder than Goodman realized, because they were secretly moonlighting on other projects without telling him. But Goodman had his little secret, too, namely that Joe and Jack were being shortchanged on their share of the profits from Captain America. They would discover the truth, ironically, from Martin's own accountant, whom some people said held stock in a company owned by one of Martin's competitors. All in all, the situation at Timely was a time bomb waiting to explode. When it did, Simon and Kirby left for National Comics, which offered them a fabulous $500 a week to work on* Boy Commandos *and* Sandman, *among others.*

Of course, luck seems to deal most of the cards in the game of life. One of the early hands dealt to me was a surprisingly unexpected development. When Joe and Jack left Timely in 1941, since I was the only other one in the department, Martin put me in charge "temporarily" until he could find a replacement. I assume he wanted to find someone who wasn't just out of his teens to wear the mantle of editor. But apparently he had a short interest span and eventually stopped looking.

So there I was, Mr. Timely Comics, and I hadn't even turned nineteen. In some ways, I was embarrassed to let visitors to the office know that I was the editor because they might think we weren't a serious business if an eighteen-year-old kid was running the shop. Sometimes I'd be in the reception room and some grown-up would come in and see me sitting there in my sneakers and sweatshirt, and say, "Hey, kid, where can I find Mr. Lee?" It would always embarrass me, because I knew he himself would be embarrassed if I said, "I'm Mr. Lee." So instead, I'd say, "Just a minute, sir, I'll tell him you're here." Then I'd run out and call the receptionist, "Tell him Mr. Lee is gone for the day." Of course, I couldn't keep doing that for long.

Here's an example of my brilliant business acumen. We turned out comicbooks about the Sub-Mariner and the Human Torch that sold for ten cents each in those days. Today, a mint-

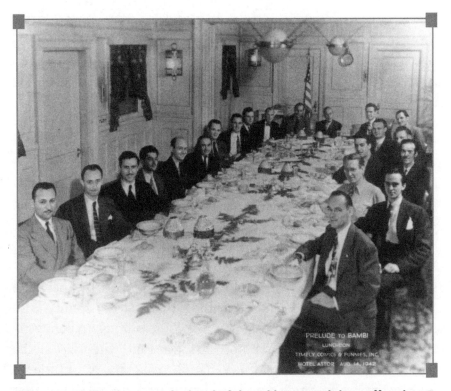

When Martin Goodman, at the head of the table, treated the staff to dinner and a movie we were too busy smiling at the camera to eat. I'm the guy with the sappy grin, four men removed from Martin's right.

condition copy of either one is worth in the neighborhood of $20,000 to $25,000, which is not a bad neighborhood. The example I promised you? I never saved a single copy.

Timely put out a variety of comicbooks with all sorts of characters. Martin's mandate was to keep the stories simple enough to be understood by young children. All the reading and the countless movies I had seen helped me to dream up the kind of stories he wanted without too much trouble. After all, they were simple plots. We're not talking *War and Peace* here. In fact, I was probably the ultimate, quintessential hack. If Westerns were the popular thing, I wrote Western scripts. If mysteries were what Martin thought would sell, mysteries were what I wrote. The same was true of romance stories, horror tales, teenage humor, whatever. And there were always other competent freelancers to write the scripts that I didn't have time to handle.

While revealing a precocious facility for the comicbook format, Stan's early adventures in the realm of imagination were soon interrupted by the reality of life in places he had never given any thought to, places like Pearl Harbor and Bataan. World War II had started!

I asked myself, "What am I doing here, writing comicbooks?" I answered, "I don't know." I felt I had to get into the army, be a hero like Errol Flynn (my favorite heroic buckler of swash) or John Wayne ("Yup" with cowboy boots). So I enlisted. I used to go to penny arcades in New York and shoot those little guns and win prizes all the time—I figured I was a shoo-in to handle real guns. What little we know when we're young. I enlisted in the army because I couldn't bear the idea of my being home while other guys my age were fighting. I don't think I could have lived with myself if I hadn't enlisted. To tell you the truth, I was actually kind of scared—but I didn't want to think of myself as a coward or a slacker.

My parents were worried about me when I enlisted, the way any parents would be, but they didn't try to stop me. I had been making my own decisions for quite a while by that time. Martin wasn't happy about my leaving, but I found a friend to replace me, an artist named Vince Fago who had been doing great work on our animated cartoon comics, and I assured Martin that Vince would do a fine job—which I think he did. Anyway, Martin knew he had no choice and, in those days, it was considered unpatriotic to try to talk anyone out of joining the service.

Besides, I was sure I'd be back soon. Hey, how long could it take us to defeat one little island nation?

War and the Writer

In the winter of 1942, Stan found himself in the service, along with millions of others. He had his basic training at the Signal Corps at Fort Monmouth, an army base in New Jersey. After that, he waited to be sent overseas where he expected to be working with the combat troops, maintaining and repairing the lines of communication. Stan was fired up with excitement, anticipating the adventure of climbing telephone poles and splicing wire under fire. Even then, he seemed to see things in comicbook form.

It was mid-winter. Being from New York, I was reasonably used to cold winters and was sure New Jersey couldn't be much colder; after all, it was only one state south of New York. How much colder could New Jersey be? Well, I soon got my answer. My first assignment at Fort Monmouth was to stand guard duty at night, there in sight of the Atlantic Ocean. Young as I was, they couldn't fool me. I was aware nobody was expecting an instant invasion on the Jersey shore and I was really just placed there for training, to toughen me up. I wasn't sure how cooling my heels at the shore for a few hours would toughen me up, but since I had nothing better to do at that time, I had no problem with it. Just a piece of cake, thought I. But after the first half hour, once the sun went down and the frigid wind came up, I turned into one human ice-cube of a sentry. When the next victim

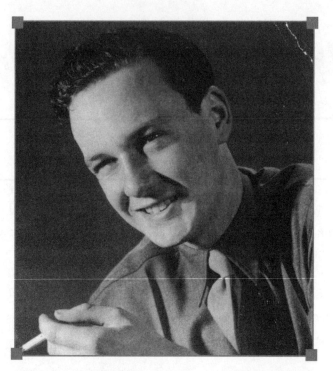

Chapter 3

1943. I was probably the only noncom who didn't smoke.
Inhaling made me cough. But I did so wanna look
like Humphrey Bogart.

finally showed up to relieve me, I raced back to the barracks so fast
that I almost caused a sonic boom.

Reaching the barracks, I ran over to the red-hot potbellied
stove and stood so close to it that my brand-new uniform, coat
and all, caught on fire. Every time I hear the term "Sad Sack," I feel
like suing, because that character was undeniably based on me.

*As day after day went by, Stan began to fear he'd spend the rest of the
war keeping America safe by serving guard duty on the coast of New
Jersey. However, he was soon due for a surprise.*

Unexpectedly, new orders came in. Stan was being transferred to a special Signal Corps unit back in New York. It seems someone at headquarters had learned he was a scriptwriter and one was needed at the Signal Corps' Training Film Division, in Astoria, Queens.

I couldn't believe it. The army felt it had found something even more important for me to do than guarding New Jersey from an impending enemy invasion. They wanted me to write training films. It wasn't till I was discharged three years later that I learned, when I read my discharge certificate, that the army, in its infinite wisdom, had actually classified me not as a highly trained, combat-ready signal corps specialist—but as a playwright! Not quite the macho image I had longed for, but I learned to live with it.

I also learned that there were only eight other men in the U.S. Army with that particular military occupational specialty (MOS) classification besides me. One of them was Frank Capra, another was William Saroyan, another Charles Addams, the great *New Yorker* cartoonist who inspired the *Addams Family* TV series. Still others were Ivan Goff and Ben Roberts, who would later achieve fame as the screenwriters of *White Heat, Captain Horatio Hornblower, King of the Khyber Rifles,* and *Man of a Thousand Faces,* among others. As if that wasn't enough, in 1976 they created the TV hit *Charlie's Angels.*

And there I was, a humble comicbook scribe, who by that time was finally earning a whole dollar a page for my labors. There could be only one explanation for my inclusion in that august group. They must have felt they needed one token nonentity in the crowd. I guess political correctness mattered even then. Of course, I eventually made my mark in the world, though I've no idea what happened to poor Capra and Saroyan and the others.

Stan spent the next three years being shipped to various army posts in several states, including North Carolina and Indiana. He was writing

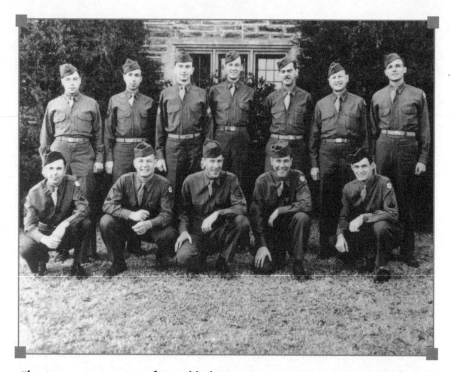

That's me, center rear of my old platoon. You never saw nicer guys, but in my imagination I was Lee Marvin and we were *The Dirty Dozen*.

instructional manuals as well as scripts for training films, and even drawing an occasional poster, all in the interest of educating the troops. While he never illustrated comics at Timely, he drew a number of posters for the army. He had always secretly wanted to be an artist, among all his other ambitions, which was another reason why he liked the comicbook business. Of course, doing posters was easier than comics. One drawing and you were finished.

As for my brilliant scripting work in the army, it wasn't the expected Bam! Zap! Pow! sort of thing. It was far more sophisticated, with classic themes such as *The G.I. Method of Organizing a Footlocker*. In true army fashion, many of the films I was assigned to write dealt with subjects I knew absolutely nothing about, such as *The Nomenclature and Operation of a 16mm Eyemo Camera Under Combat Conditions.* Me, who had trouble focusing a Kodak Brownie. But somehow, just like the army itself, I managed to muddle through.

My modus operandi was to study the training manuals carefully and then try to simplify them for the films and film strips I wrote, the purpose being to make the instructions easy for the recruits to understand. Or, I often wrote entire training manuals in the form of comicbooks. It was an excellent way of educating and communicating, and I just wish I had copies of those now. Not anticipating that decades later the world would be excitedly clamoring for my biography, just as with my earliest comicbooks, I never thought to save any of them.

Along with Stan, several other comicbook artists and writers served in the military, including Joe Simon, Jack Kirby, Bill Everett, and Carl Burgos, while in the civilian world Timely Comics was now booming with all sorts of new titles. Their lineup included lighter reading, humorous comics, and issues appealing to girls, such as Patsy Walker, Miss America, Mighty Mouse, *and many others. It was the booming Golden Age of Comics.*

At Timely, Martin Goodman hired new staffers and supplemented their work with the contributions of his freelancers who were in the army. He could certainly afford to do so. By the middle of the war, publishers were selling 25 million comicbooks a month.

I've always been a fast writer, mainly because of my impatience and wanting to get finished as soon as possible. Also, I'm a gregarious guy. I like being with people, talking to people, even arguing with people. But I can't do it when I'm writing. Writing is about as lonely an activity as you can find. Even at home, my friends know not to disturb me when I'm writing, nor can I write and fool around with my wife at the same time. I just sit alone in a room pounding on keys. Of course, one good thing about it is, it's cheaper than psychiatry. I can always take my frustrations out on those helpless little keys.

Now why did I bring that up? Oh, yeah—so I wrote my little training films and instructional manuals the same as I've always written everything else, as fast as I could. I never expected that one day the officer in charge would tell me to take it easy because the others in our unit were turning out their material at a slower pace and I was making it look as if they were dragging their feet. Well, since I had to slow down, that left me with lots of spare time on my hands, and it was then that an idea hit me. If there wasn't enough military work for me, I decided to outmaneuver the army by doing freelance scripts for Timely Comics. Unlike many men who went to war, I didn't leave my job—I took it with me.

In time, Stan was transferred to Duke University, where army units were billeted and the services of a training-film writer were needed. While there, Stan fulfilled one dream he'd had since those days when he was a kid and it seemed that only the doctors' families owned cars. He could now afford to buy a '36 Plymouth, his first automobile. The fact that it wasn't just a secondhand car but rather a thirdhand heap didn't bother him at all. He paid twenty dollars for it and felt like a king. He particularly enjoyed one of its special features. The one-piece vertical windshield was hinged at the top. If Stan turned a knob on the dashboard, the windshield lifted outward from the bottom until it flattened horizontally, parallel with the roof, so the wind could blow into the car. It was like having a semi-convertible with all the insects flying in his face, and he loved every minute of it.

With growing ambition, I decided that now that I owned a '36 Plymouth, it was time for me to become an officer. Thinking back now, I'm not sure of the connection, but it seemed to make sense at that time. Unfortunately, when I applied for officer's candidate school (OCS), my commanding officer wouldn't approve my application.

He said, "Stan, if you become an officer, we'll lose you. They'll send you overseas. And we don't have enough writers to do all our instructional manuals and films."

By that time I wasn't thinking of instructional manuals and films. I was picturing myself in a great-looking officer's uniform with bars on my shoulders, bars that would make me a magnet to females. So I said, "But I want to go overseas! It's my duty. The army needs more officers!"

He sighed impatiently, returned my dejected salute, turned on his heel and marched away. And that was that. My chance to become a war hero and have women swooning at my feet had just gone up in smoke. The irony of it was, I was soon given the rank of corporal, then I made sergeant, and wouldja believe I was ordered to help train combat troops. Me, who had never even been out of the country!

So picture this: I was about nineteen or twenty years old, a skinny kid from New York whose military job was writing instructional books and films. Yet, I was also supposed to give orientation lectures to troops who were returning from tours of duty in Europe so that they'd be prepared for what they'd encounter when they went to the Orient. Yep, rough, tough ol' Sarge Lee would give 'em the benefit of his experience and combat-wise savvy!

I felt like the world's biggest phony. But, in an effort to seem credible to those great, battle-scarred guys, I wore dirty fatigues, kept my sleeves rolled up like John Wayne, always had a few days' growth of stubble on my face, used plenty of cuss words when I talked, and even tried to spit a lot, as if I was chewing tobacco, in a desperate effort to look as rugged as I could.

It made *me* feel better—but I've a hunch I didn't fool one single G.I.

Later, I got transferred to Fort Benjamin Harrison in Indiana, where one of my stellar contributions to the war effort was to write the marching song for the Army Finance Department. Yes, Virginia, there really was an Army Finance Department. Somebody had to do the payrolls, and those office commandos needed instruction films as much as the others. As I'd watch them marching around the field with a sergeant drilling them, it seemed to me they weren't the most spirited group I'd ever seen. I felt they needed their own marching song to bolster their morale.

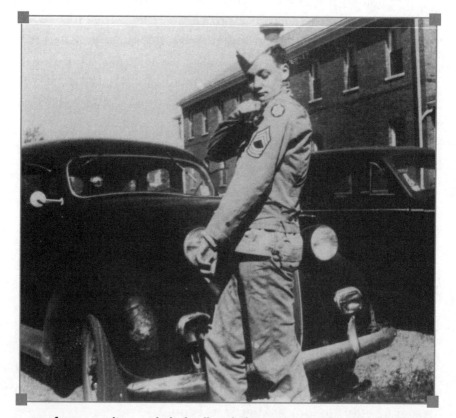

My first car, a battered ol' thirdhand Plymouth. But I felt it befitted a master sergeant, so I borrowed my top-kick's jacket to pose in.

So I wrote one for them. Not knowing how to write music, I simply penned lyrics to match the "Air Force Song." It caught on big-time. They started singing it in cadence while they marched. For all I know, it might have become the official anthem of the fighting Finance Department. And now, here it is, for the world to thrill to:

> Off we go, into our office yonder,
>   At our desks, morning 'til night.
> Far away from any battle's thunder,
>   We pay off the fellas who fight.
> Clerks alert, guarding our books from blunder,
>   Payroll forms clutter the floor.
> We write, compute, sit tight, don't shoot.
>   Nothing can stop the Fiscal D'rector.

Perhaps to show their undying appreciation, the Finance Department gave Stan a new assignment. It happened because they felt they weren't training payroll officers quickly enough. That was hurting morale in cases where G.I.s weren't getting paid on time. Just like on Mission: Impossible, *Stan's task, if he'd accept it, was to rewrite the payroll manuals so that the courses could be taught more quickly and more payroll officers could be sent into the field. Though he knew as much about army finance as he did about brain surgery, Stan pored over the existing manuals and rewrote much of the material in the form of cartoons and puzzles. He created a character called Fiscal Freddy and made up a game where one had to guide Freddy through a maze (the maze consisting of payroll procedures) without making any mistakes and without crossing any lines. By turning a dry subject into a fun experience, Stan's project considerably reduced the time it took to train and prepare payroll officers for duty.*

Clearly, Fiscal Freddy and I won the war single-handedly! Think of it: what if the military drivers at Yalta had refused to drive Churchill, Stalin, and Roosevelt around because their paychecks hadn't arrived on time? Those were serious issues, and in my own humble way I feel I helped save the Republic from disaster by addressing them head-on. Aside to members of the Congressional Medal of Honor Committee—my number's in the phone book.

But things didn't always go smoothly. One time I got into a jam that almost ended up with me being sentenced to Leavenworth! And if that isn't a great attention-getter, then I give up. Anyway, here's how it happened . . .

As I mentioned earlier, I spent some of my spare time—which consisted mainly of the late evening hours—writing comics for Timely because they still wanted my stuff, which was very flattering, and I wanted the extra money, which was very greedy. The system we worked out was simplicity itself. They'd send me letters in care of the APO on my base, telling me what stories they needed and when they were needed, and then I'd write them and mail them back as soon as possible to meet Timely's publishing deadlines. Few things in publishing are more important than meeting deadlines.

So here's where the Leavenworth factor came in. I knew I was supposed to receive a letter on Friday giving me my next writing assignment, which was due next Tuesday. So I planned to write it over the weekend, mail it Monday, and they'd receive it Tuesday, right on time. When Friday's mail call came around the mail clerk didn't sing out my name. I couldn't understand it. Timely never missed a mailing. So I asked the mail clerk, "Are you sure there's no letter for me?"

"Nah, nothin'." He wasn't the most communicative noncom in the regiment.

Next day was Saturday. The mail room was closed and locked. As I was walking past it, I just happened to glance through the window and I could see, in the *L* cubbyhole inside, an envelope

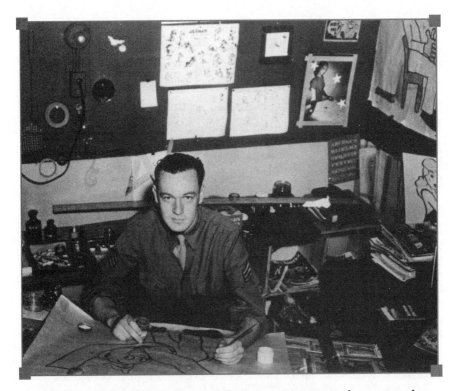

Here it is, proof positive that the ol' sarge was winning the war single-handedly by drawing cartoons for the whole free world.

with the Timely return address clearly visible. The letter had been there all the time!

I was young, hot-tempered, and annoyed at the army and the war for interfering with my career, so I did just what any comic-book hero would have done. I marched back to the company clerk and demanded that he open the locked mail room for me. He calmly dismissed me with a wave of his hand. It was Saturday. The mail room was locked on Saturdays and that was that. I said, "But there's a letter for me inside that I need. I saw it in the *L* cubbyhole. Look, is it okay if I open the lock myself?" It was a simple padlock on a hinge. All I'd need was a screwdriver to unscrew the hinge, open the door, and then screw the hinge back on again. Wouldn't even have to open the lock itself. The ever-alert company clerk mumbled something that sounded to me like "Okay" and returned to his nap.

So I took a screwdriver, walked to the mail room, unscrewed the hinge holding the padlock, opened the door, took my letter, and then locked everything up again. I opened the letter, took note of my writing assignment, batted out the script that weekend, mailed it to Timely on Monday so it would arrive on Tuesday, and forgot about the incident. Until the next day!

I received an order to report to the company commander's office on the double. I think it was the first "on the double" order I'd ever gotten. We army writers were seldom needed for anything that quickly.

When I reached his office (on the double) the company commander, a captain who had always thought of me as a wise-guy New Yorker, accused me of robbing the mail. I told him I had only taken my own letter and then closed everything up very neatly. He wasn't impressed. He seemed to enjoy telling me that mail robbery was a federal offense, even for wise-guy New Yorkers, as I would soon learn during my stay at Leavenworth.

Stan was in deep trouble and almost brought up on charges. Happily for him, the colonel for whom Stan had written the training manual for finance officers didn't want to lose his one Signal Corps writer. The captain was promptly ordered to forget the whole matter and to concentrate on winning the war, and Stan was off the hook.

Shortly thereafter I got one of my all-time strangest assignments. It had to do with venereal disease.

Now I'll confess to you, in confidence, that I'm not the greatest authority on venereal disease. So I was somewhat surprised when I was told to create and illustrate a poster about the subject.

It seems the army was having a problem. Enlisted men overseas were often enjoying carnal knowledge of the opposite sex without availing themselves of the proper safeguards. (And if anyone can convey that same intelligence more delicately, I take off my hat to him.) The army found that after their brief period of indescribable ecstasy, too many enlisted men were contracting syphilis. Because of that, the military had set up what they called prophylactic stations all over Europe. After their fling in the hay, the enlisted men—and I don't know why it was only the enlisted men who were singled out; perhaps it was felt that, in the case of officers, no germ would dare—the enlisted men were supposed to go to one of those pro stations and submit to a procedure that, in the name of delicacy, I won't describe, the purpose of which was to protect them from getting a venereal disease. Those little pro stations dotted the landscape, with small green lights above the entrances to make them easily recognizable.

So what did that have to do with the ol' sarge? Well, I was asked to create a poster that would remind and encourage enlisted men to go to a pro station after they had been overzealous in the romance department. I'll admit I was a little disappointed that I wasn't ordered to go overseas and seek out some of those women of easy virtue personally, in order to do firsthand research for the poster project, but you can't win 'em all.

I must have sketched countless complex, meaningful, persuasive, intellectual ideas for an anti-VD poster, but nothing seemed right. Then, when I least expected it, inspiration hit me. The simplest idea of all. I merely drew a little cartoon version of a happy-looking G.I. walking into a pro station, with the little green light above the door, wearing a proud expression on his face and a dialogue balloon over his head that read, *"VD? Not me!"*

Well, they must have printed a zillion of those posters and displayed them all over Europe. Due to me, the majority of our enlisted men were probably saved from becoming venereal victims. But did I get a presidential citation? A medal? Even a complimentary box of condoms? I love the army—but how soon they forget!

During my last year in service, I traded in the Plymouth and bought a Buick convertible with the money I had made writing scripts. It was jet black with red leather seats and whitewall tires. It was the most beautiful vehicle I had ever seen, a symphony on four wheels. It was also one of the few four-door convertibles made and, since it was years before the advent of push-button tops, due to the many wing nuts and bolts that had to be manipulated to put the top up and down, the process took about an hour, even with someone helping me. But it was worth it to be able to drive around the post in that incredible motorized vision. I might add that I bought the car secondhand, which was the reason I could afford it, but its age in no way diminished its luster in my eyes.

Naturally, it was a real girl magnet so I was never lacking for dates during the months that I owned it, although I tried to convince myself that it was my inherent charm and machismo that really did the trick.

One last story before I take you back to civilian life. It involves Harry Stonehill, a good friend I had in the service who tried to dissuade me from returning to the world of comicbooks after the war. Harry was a lieutenant and a former businessman from Chicago. When peace was declared and we were about to be mustered out, he said, "Stan, after we're discharged, how about coming to the Philippines with me?"

I thought he was nuts. "Why would I want to go to the Philippines? I'm heading back to New York, to my job with the comicbooks."

"But I found out they don't have Christmas cards in the Philippines. I'm gonna buy a heap of Christmas cards and go there and make a ton of money. We can be partners," Harry insisted.

I said, "You're a lunatic."

Well, the lunatic went to the Philippines with a ton of Xmas cards. A few months later, I got a letter from him. He had set up his

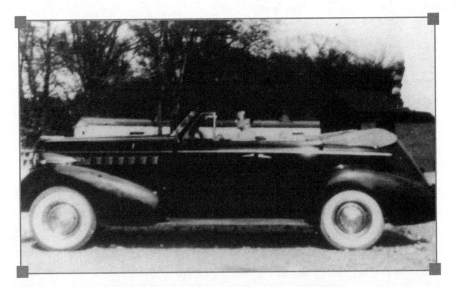

Okay, so it was old. But it was black as night with big white tires and scarlet red leather seats and it was mine, all mine!

own business and was doing very well. I figured, good for him. He must have a nice little greeting-card shop on an island somewhere. As the months and years went by I kept hearing from Harry. It seemed he now owned the franchise for U.S. Tobacco. Then I learned he had built a large glass-manufacturing company. Next time I heard he had created a fast-growing import-export company. It went on and on. Bottom line: After a few years my old army pal, Harry, had become the wealthiest man in the Philippines!

I remember once writing to him and asking, "What kind of car are you driving?" because we always used to talk about cars. He wrote back, "Stan, I own half of the cars here in the Philippines. I've got dealerships."

Yep, any time my ego needs deflating, I remember how I was too smart to leave my comicbooks and go into business with ol' Harry!

Return to Wonderland

When the war ended, Stan skipped an orientation lecture on how to be a civilian again—he was pretty clear on that already. It was 1945, and he was out of the army and headed home to a job he loved. Stan didn't even take a vacation, but headed right back to Timely Comics and the friends he had worked with before.

But work wasn't the only thing on his mind those first few weeks . . .

I was mustered out of the army in Indianapolis. Five minutes after receiving my discharge papers, I was in my convertible heading for New York. I somehow didn't feel I needed to stay for the one-hour orientation lecture that the army offered for the purpose of helping me readjust to civilian life. I'd been a civilian most of my life; I didn't think it would be that hard for me to get back into the swing of things.

A civilian once more, I took a two-room apartment at the Alamac Hotel on Broadway and Seventy-first Street, while trying to decide where I'd really want to live permanently. One day, while coming down in the elevator in the Alamac, I saw this gorgeous blonde who looked like a young Lauren Bacall—very classy looking. She was carrying a box with the name Saks Fifth Avenue on it. I had the feeling she was taking a garment to the store, possibly to return it.

ENLISTED RECORD AND REPORT OF SEPARATION
HONORABLE DISCHARGE *DETACHED ENLISTED MEN'S LIST*

[Military discharge form for Lieber, Stanley M., Sgt, with handwritten annotations "WRONG" near Writer occupation, and arrow pointing to "Playwright 288"]

With the military classification "playwright," it wasn't easy
convincing girls that I was a hard-bitten war hero.

As any young, red-blooded vet would, I began following her
right on to a Fifth Avenue bus that she took, headed downtown. It
wasn't something I wanted to do, it was something I *had* to do. It
was my duty as a new male civilian, and besides, I just had to know
who she was.

The bus was crowded and we both had to stand. Naturally I
managed to stand right next to her. Summoning up all my nerve, I
struck up a conversation, feeling just a little bit surprised at how
readily she became friendly with a stranger. But of course I attrib-

uted that to my innate charm. Sure enough, I learned she was on her way to return something at Saks. So, being the gentleman I was, I offered to carry the box for her and accompanied her to the store, because . . . well, actually I didn't need a reason.

One thing led to another and we ended up back at the hotel where she asked if I'd like to come up to her room with her.

She didn't look like the kind of girl who would say that, at least not after knowing me for a half hour. But, once again, I attributed it to my irresistible appeal, and we went upstairs.

We hit it off great together and became good friends. The reason I know we hit it off so well is because she didn't ask for any payment. It turned out she was a very high-priced lady who was, to put it as gallantly as possible, in business for herself.

Often, when it seemed we were running out of conversation, she'd tell me about the men she dated and about their particular sexual proclivities. I became one of the best-informed people about the world of erotic experiences, even though those torrid tidbits of information were, on my part, mostly gained second-hand. And, as attractive as she was, I'm sure it's clear to the observant reader that we remained together for many months mainly because of my unquenchable thirst for knowledge.

The only letdown during those days came when I traded in the Buick convertible for a brand-new white sedan. Much as I loved that attention-getting black car, the weather in New York wasn't conducive for a convertible. Not enough warm sunny days, and even when the weather was just right, it took forever to put the top down. I was inordinately proud of my new white sedan because it was the first car I owned that I hadn't bought secondhand. I couldn't wait to take my mother and my aunt Mitzi for a drive. My parents had never owned a car and I thought Mom would be thrilled, but she was so busy talking to Aunt Mitzi all during the ride that she never even mentioned the car as we drove around. It was like somebody hanging around the room while the Super Bowl is on TV and not asking what the score is. But hey, that's women for you. Luckily, there were plenty of females to whom I wasn't related who gave me the requisite amount of attention when we went joy riding.

Those were good days for Stan. He had an interesting job, a few bucks in his pocket, a new white sedan—and the city was filled with beautiful, single females. Not surprisingly, when Stan would later start creating new superhero characters, they would all have qualities he remembered and possessed in his own life. For one thing, Stan was the quintessential native of the same town where many of his heroes would live—New York City.

The Alamac Hotel where I lived was about forty blocks north of our offices in the Empire State Building. Inasmuch as I love to walk, I'd usually walk to work. I could average a block a minute, so I allowed myself an hour and ten minutes to get to work and was almost always on time. A little leg weary perhaps, but on time. In fact, I rarely took a cab, subway, or bus anywhere at all. I walked all over New York. Even years later, when our office was on Fifty-seventh and Madison, if I had to take some people down to Greenwich Village, which was about sixty blocks away, everyone would say, "Let's grab a cab." But I'd try to get them to walk because I knew that sixty blocks would take about an hour while the cab would take almost that long during rush hour and our only exercise would be watching the meter go up and up.

I still remember two very close friends of mine who worked with me some years later, Sol Brodsky and Stan Goldberg. We'd often have lunch together and I can prove what good friends they were because they would never fail to walk with me to restaurants I chose that were at least a mile away, even though they griped and complained every step of the way.

I've been thin most if not all of my life. Often people would ask what I did to stay in shape and I'd answer honestly, "I walk

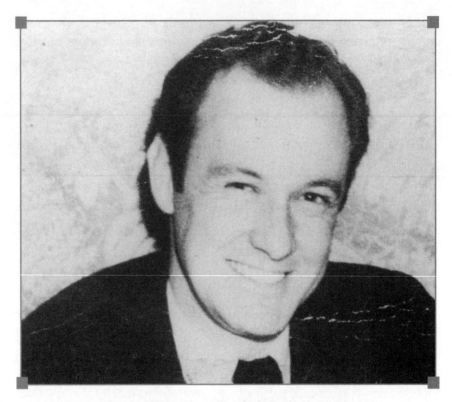

I kept walking around with this ridiculous grin
after I met Joanie, my wife-to-be.

whenever possible instead of taking public transportation." I could
tell nobody believed me. They'd always add, "No, seriously, do you
play golf, tennis, jog, go to the gym, what?" Finally, I'd simply say
that I attributed my inability to gain weight to worry. But not casual worry. It had to be a period of intensive, regimented worry-
ing, at least an hour a day, uninterrupted. Wouldja believe more
people accepted that wacky explanation than the truth about
walking?

Occasionally I'd interrupt my walk to the Empire State Building to do something else I enjoyed. My route took me along Central
Park West and in those days they had stables located there that pro-

vided horses for the park's bridal path. So I'd sometimes leave the hotel early in order to stop over and rent a horse, ride around the park, bring it back to the stable, and then continue my walk to work.

There was one horse that was my favorite, Red Man. He was huge, the biggest horse I ever saw, and I felt like Roy Rogers on him. He wasn't a racehorse, but he ran real fast. Galloping was forbidden in the park and that really frustrated me. So one day I hit upon a sinister scheme. As soon as I saw a mounted policeman patrolling the bridal path, I tapped Red Man with my heels, urging him to gallop. As expected, the cop called out to me, "Hey, son, slow down. No galloping!"

Instead of slowing down, I urged Red Man to go even faster, while shouting back to the officer at the same time, "I can't stop him. He's running away with me! Help!" All the time I was prodding the horse to make him go faster.

The cop yelled back, "Hold on, son! Don't panic! I'll come after you!"

So he starting chasing behind while we galloped all around the park at top speed, with me yelling, "Hurry, Officer, I can't stop him!"

Finally, we got near to where the stables were and I reined Red Man to a stop.

"Gee, Officer, thanks a lot," I said, as he came up beside me. "If you hadn't been following me, I sure would have been scared."

"Well, you did very well, son. Lucky you didn't fall off. You've got to be careful. Don't ride such an uncontrollable horse next time. Get a more gentle one."

"Yes, sir. I'll be sure to do that. Thanks again, Officer."

A wave of the hand and he trotted off. That was one helluva nice cop. As for me, I had the satisfaction of knowing that even a mounted patrolman's horse couldn't catch up to good ol' Red Man. I guess that's about as close as I ever came to being a dedicated lawbreaker, and I only mention it now because I'm assuming the statute of limitations will protect me.

Another thing about Central Park. The Central Park lake was my social arena. To me, it represented total romance. My idea of the ideal date was to take a girl out in a rowboat on the lake. I'm a pretty good rower—almost any guy is, since it's not all that hard to row a rowboat—but I still felt like a real hunk with a girl facing me and watching admiringly (or so I thought) as I skillfully navigated the dangerous waters of that small, ever-calm lake.

I also loved walking in the park. In those days you weren't as apt to be mugged. So I'd often take a date to Central Park, walk along the paths, linger at the zoo, treat her to some peanuts, go for a row, and after that—it's none of your business. Yep, to me New York provided the best and most inexpensive ways for a couple to have a great time.

The other thing I loved to do was take bus rides at night. They used to have those great, big, slow, double-decker buses that rode all around Manhattan for only a dime. Next to rowing, I thought it was the most romantic date you could have, sitting real high on top of the bus in one of the cozy back seats. I'd put my arm around the girl (I was a real daredevil in those days) and we would have the whole island of Manhattan plus the Jersey shore as our backdrop. Best of all, the ride took at least a couple of hours.

So there I was, young, single, living in the greatest city in the world, a city that had more than its share of places to go, things to do, and girls, girls, girls. It couldn't get any better than that.

Whoa! I almost forgot another wonderful thing about life back then. When I think about it, it seems totally fantastic to me now, but in the forties it was actually commonplace. You'll probably have trouble believing this.

You know how crowded New York is today. In fact every big city is pretty much the same. It's almost impossible to find a parking space, mainly because there are so few parking spaces left. In most big cities, if you keep your own car, you're even lucky to find a parking garage that you can afford on a monthly basis. I can testify that it costs more to garage a car for a month in Manhattan now than it did to rent a luxury apartment back then.

But here's the unbelievable situation that I experienced while living at the Hotel Alamac. There was a parking garage on West End Avenue, about two blocks from the hotel. I had the following arrangement with them. Whenever I wanted my car, they would drive it from the garage, with a little motorcycle attached to the back, and leave it parked for me in front of the hotel. Then the man who left it for me would detach the motorcycle and ride it back to the garage. It was no problem because there were places to park on every street at that time—and no parking meters.

Later, when I finished using the car, I had only to leave it parked anywhere near the hotel. Their men on motorcycles were always cruising around, and when one would spot it he'd simply drive it back to the garage for me. The garage's customers all had little identifying stickers that were pasted on our windshields so that the motorcycle valets could always spot our cars.

Now, as if that service wasn't incredible enough, here's the pièce de résistance. We customers were charged the staggering sum of twelve dollars a month for all that, and I forgot to mention that they also washed the car every time it was returned to the garage.

Of course, human nature being what it is, most people, including me, were too dumb to appreciate a deal like that. I was always scanning the ads in the paper to see if I could get a better rate somewhere else.

A Happy Hack Once More

The 1940s and 1950s were a time of great tension in America, even if they now seem to be "The Good Old Days." Although we had just won a global war and industry was shifting to massive civilian production, and the future looked rosy, still huge social and personal changes were taking place. Couples who had delayed marriage because of the war were rushing into matrimony, forming new families who would eventually become the baby boomers and Stan's future readers.

Overseas, some of our wartime allies—mostly in Europe—were destitute. Other allies were becoming our philosophical and political enemies, spying on us and trying to subvert us and threaten us with nuclear destruction. They would also supply Stan and his colleagues with new villains for their stories.

But for the time being, few people enjoyed living in New York more than Stan, even though he knew that everything wasn't all fun and games. Though he was happy with the work he was doing, he still had to contend with life's ever-present problems.

While I really enjoyed my job and the stories I was writing, there was one thing that both irritated and frustrated me. It was the fact that nobody, outside of our own little circle, had a good word to say about comicbooks. To the public at large, comics were at the very bottom of the cultural totem pole. Most of the adult world didn't buy them, care about them, or want their children to "waste their time reading them."

I remember at parties guests would walk over to me and say, "What do you do?" Knowing how most people felt about comics, I'd try to avoid giving the sordid details and merely reply, "Oh, I'm a writer." Then I'd start walking away before more probing questions could be asked. But often the person would follow me and add, "But what do you write?" I'd still attempt to evade the issue by answering, "Stories for young people." But often the other party was too persistent. "What kind of stories?" By now I'd be getting desperate. "For, eh, various magazines," would be my cowardly reply. But it was usually a losing battle. At some point I'd have to own up and say, "I write comicbooks." At that exact instant my interrogator's voice would lose its interest and the tone would become distinctly distant as he or she would utter the inevitable words, "Oh, I see," and turn and walk away as if I had a communicable disease.

I tried to tell myself that it wasn't all that bad because the next day I'd be immersed in a world of fantasy and imagination, doing work that was fun and absorbing, while many of the people who denigrated comics couldn't make that claim for themselves.

Personally, I was never consumed by what I wrote. While I got a kick out of doing comics, it was just a job to me. I'd never been the kind of writer who was always thinking of things to write. Being the ultimate hack, I would start doing my thinking when I sat down in front of the typewriter, and not a minute before. Because, when I wasn't actually writing, my thoughts were centered on far more important things, like movies, sports, and girls. So, since I didn't consider comics the be-all and end-all of my existence, I was able to live with the fact that the outside world would never be impressed by the work I was doing.

Anyway, there was so much going on that there wasn't time for a lot of introspection. Things were booming at Timely after the

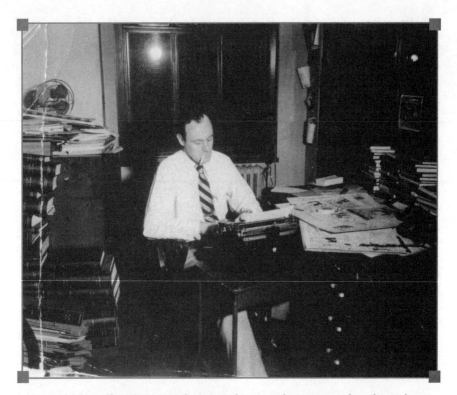

Once again, when I saw a photographer nearby, I popped a phony butt in my mouth, trying to look like my friend Mickey Spillane.

war. There were no more paper shortages, so publishers could print as many copies of as many issues as they wanted. The public, after years of deprivation and hardship, was desperate for entertainment. There was a mood of excitement at our company and everyone was in a state of high energy.

Besides producing the usual type of comicbook stories, I tried to expand our market, to do books that would appeal to girls as well as boys. I could never understand why comicbooks were primarily a boys' market and I wanted to try to change that. After all, I thought, everyone always likes a good story. So I began to produce titles featuring humorous, romantic stories that I felt would appeal to females, titles like *Millie the Model, Tessie the Typist, Nellie the Nurse,* and *Hedy of Hollywood.* It's obvious that I was attempting to cover every field that I felt would be of interest to girls. But, just so it wouldn't seem we were in a rut, I also introduced a new adventurous superheroine called *The Blonde Phantom. The Blonde Phantom* did pretty well for about three years, by which time we launched three more superheroine books, *Namora, Sun Girl,* and *Venus.*

However, it became clear to me that the market for female heroes was really minimal. The new titles, while action-packed and well illustrated, just didn't catch on the way we had hoped they would. I finally realized that girls would never be a large enough audience for superhero (or superheroine) thrillers, just as boys would never be as large a market for Barbie dolls.

The next thing we tried, in an effort to expand our readership, was combining some of our major superheroes into groups. In 1946, we pulled together Captain America, the Human Torch, Sub-Mariner, Miss America, and the Whizzer into something we called *The All Winners Squad,* which I thought was a great idea. It had only one shortcoming: It didn't sell. To this day I don't know why. Anyway, we dumped it after two issues.

To my dismay, the age of the superheroes seemed to be drawing to a close, and we began phasing them out. We began to fear that we might be exiting the so-called Golden Age of Comics.

We, and all the other publishers, tried everything we could to find a formula that would work in the postwar market. We tried doing comics featuring funny animals, and took a fling at teen humor, romance, true crime, and Westerns. All anyone had to do was name a category and we slapped a few comics together in that department. Nothing became a break-out hit but we didn't stop trying and, at least, we were paying our way.

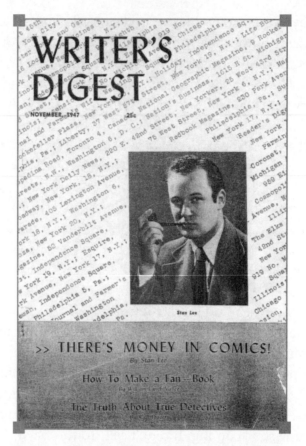

Stan Lee

>> THERE'S MONEY IN COMICS!
By Stan Lee

How To Make a Fan—Book
By William Lauch Vance

The Truth About True Detectives
By R. J. Janners

1947. My first feature article in a real magazine.
The pipe was to make me look literary. It just made me sick.

Writer's Digest *commissioned Stan to write the lead article for its*
November 1947 issue, titled "There's Money in Comics," and they
wanted his photo for the cover. Stan was never sure why Writer's
Digest *singled him out, but he guesses one of the editors may have*
been a comicbook fan. The two things that strike Stan about that ar-
ticle now are his cover picture and his advice to budding comicbook
writers. Regarding the cover photo, Stan thought he looked too young
to speak with sufficient gravity, so he dashed out and bought a pipe,
which he held contemplatively between his lips during the photo

shoot, thinking it would lend a certain maturity to his image. Look-ing back at it now he thinks it looks inane and his wife, Joanie, is con-vinced it makes him look icky.

Yet his advice to writers was sound then and remains so now. It boiled down to these rules: (1) Have a Provocative Beginning; (2) Use Smooth Continuity from Panel to Panel; (3) Concentrate on Realistic Dialogue Which Leads to Good Characterization; (4) Maintain Sus-pense Throughout; and (5) Provide a Satisfying Ending. That pretty well sums it up the way Euripides, Shakespeare, and Hemingway did it. And, of course, it was the way Stan endeavored to do it all during his career.

From 1947 into the early 1950s, we decided to concentrate on the always dependable crime genre, with titles such as *Official True Crime Cases* (1947), *Crime Fighters* (1948), *True Complete Mystery* (1949), *Casey, Crime Photographer* (1949), *Amazing Detective Cases* (1950), *Spy Fighters* (1950), *Private Eye* (1951), *Police Action* (1954), and many others. After working on all those comics, I al-most expected that when I retired I'd be entitled to a police pen-sion.

Like so many of his comicbook characters, Stan was always having little adventures of his own. He tells of one time when he was having lunch at a restaurant called Diamond Jim's in Times Square with a coworker named Mel Blum. Mel was the art director of Timely's slick paper magazines and a good friend of Stan's. In trying to describe the size of an illustration, Stan gestured with his hands and accidentally knocked over a glass of milk that was at the edge of the table. A man in a blue suit was at the next table, and he and his suit got the full brunt of the spillage. Naturally, Stan apologized profusely and offered to pay for the suit cleaning.

A few minutes later, after Stan got the man calmed down, the waiter brought him another glass of milk and he turned to Mel to

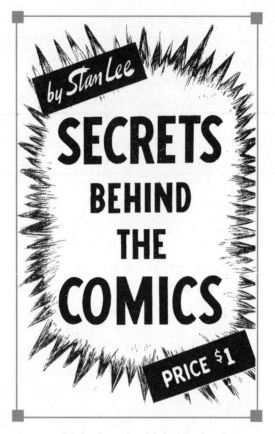

Also in '47, I wrote, published, and sold this $1 book on my own. I'll bet you'd have to pay as much as $2 for a copy today!

continue their conversation. "As I was saying," said Stan, gesturing again—and knocking over the second glass of milk—on the same man!

Together with Mel, Stan broke every known speed record racing out of there, and it's rumored he hasn't ordered a glass of milk in any restaurant ever since.

In 1949, a new trend emerged. That's the way it was with comics. One genre would be hot for a while and then another would strike fire. Almost overnight Westerns became big with the reading public. Well, there were no flies on us. We immediately dropped most of our crime titles and instead of shouting "Follow that car!" our heroes started drawling "Follow that stagecoach!"

My favorite Western was the Black Rider because he was the first of our Western superheroes. He actually had the same double-identity formula as most of our costumed superheroes. He was a peace-loving doctor in a Western town, but when the occasion arose he put on his black mask, black suit, and black cape and became the Black Rider who went out and fought the bad guys. I liked ol' Blackie so much that on one cover we decided to use a photograph of him instead of a drawing. Easy enough to do because he wore a mask that covered all of his face except for his eyes. Being the ham I am, it was I who wore the black outfit and mask and posed as the Black Rider. I've always loved that cover, even though it didn't become my ticket to a movie career as I had hoped it would.

After the Westerns, along came the war craze. Suddenly, everyone was into war stories. So, once again we leapt into galvanized action. In a short time we began to soft-pedal the Westerns and started spewing out titles such as *War Comics, Battle Comics, Battleground, Battle Brady, Combat Comics, Combat Kelly, Combat Casey,* and other similarly creative and highly imaginative titles. I sometimes felt we should change the name of our company to In a Rut Comics.

I was writing many if not most of those stories, and I'll admit I enjoyed the variety. Yet I said to myself, None of this is making an impression on anybody. We were reasonably successful, we made some money, but what bothered me was that we were always *following* the trends, never setting them. Martin Goodman would merely check the sales figures of all the various comicbook companies, see what was selling well, and then say to me, "You know, Stan, everyone else's knitting stories seem to be selling well, so let's do books about knitting." Okay, he never really asked me to do knitting books; that was just an illustration, for Pete's sake!

Then, at some later date he'd say, "The funny animal books are doing well." So we'd switch to funny animal books. It went on and on. Every few months a new trend and we'd be right there, faithfully following each one. I hated that word "following"! Even though it was a good job and I enjoyed working with all the artists and the other writers, it really wasn't creatively fulfilling. I felt that we were a company of copycats. We'd see what type of comics were selling well and then we'd flood the market with new titles in that same vein.

But it was a job, I was good at it, and things could have been worse. So I just stayed with it, occasionally wondering where it was all leading to.

I could never have imagined how it would all shake out.

Joanie at First Sight!

Her name was Joan.

She was an actress, singer, and model when Stan met her. He said she was the most gorgeous female he had ever seen, and oh, her personality. Just by saying "Hello," she could light up a room, Stan claimed. She was a blue-eyed beauty from Newcastle-on-Tyne in the north of England, and Stan swears she danced like a dream and sang like an angel. He was entranced by her charming English accent and her ability to mimic a Scotswoman, Welshwoman, Irishwoman, or even a Cockney, even though she normally spoke the King's English. According to Stan, she can still read the phone book and make it sound like a Shakespearean sonnet. She was the most talented, spectacular female he had ever seen. It was love at first sight.

When I met her, I couldn't believe any woman could be so gorgeous. I felt she could have had any man she wanted. In England, there was one fella she liked, but something happened and he married someone else. To spite him, she married the first guy that came along, an American officer, and was married to him for a few days when she realized it was a mistake. She came over to the United States as a war bride and was planning on getting a divorce when I met her.

At that time, Joanie was a successful model, specializing in hats. In those days, women were very into hats, and hat models had to be the very loveliest of all because their faces were always in close-ups. Joanie was the agency's top model and I met her quite by accident.

A cousin of mine one day told me about a model he knew and thought I might like. I was single, just out of the army, and that sounded mighty good to me.

He said her name was Betty and gave me the address of the agency where she worked.

When I went there to meet her, a stunning, drop-dead-beautiful redhead opened the door. When she spoke, her voice, in a soft, sultry English accent, ran up and down my spine.

Before I go any further, I've got to explain that I used to draw a lot when I was young and, if you're a guy and you're into drawing, chances are you'll draw pictures of pretty girls—your idealized version of pretty girls. Well, I was no exception, and the face I al-

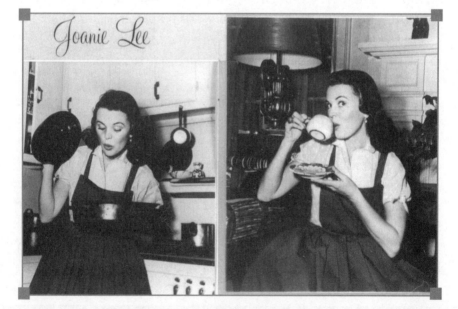

A few pix from Joanie's modeling days.
She couldn't take a bad shot if she tried.

ways drew had a tiny turned-up nose, big blue eyes, luscious lips, gorgeous hair, and a figure that never quit.

When that door opened, I was looking at the girl I had been drawing all those years. She wasn't the Betty I was supposed to meet at all—she was Joan.

I must have looked like a nut staring at her wide-eyed as she asked, "May I help you?" Those were the words she said, but what I heard in my spinning head was, "Here I am, the girl of your dreams. Don't let me get away!"

I blurted out something to the effect that I was madly in love with her. She thought I was joking and we spoke for a few minutes, and then a few minutes more, and then more. I never did get to meet Betty.

Anyway, to make a long story longer, we started dating. Shortly thereafter, I told her I wanted to marry her. She seemed to feel it was a good idea. She was about to get a divorce anyway. Since there was only a six-week wait for a divorce in Reno, that's where Joanie went. But the story doesn't end there.

She was alone in Reno for weeks, and the men out there weren't blind. That thought hit me hard at the end of the fifth week when one of her letters to me began, "Dear Jack." Now, I'm not the smartest guy in the world, but I know for sure that my name isn't Jack. Something told me I ought to fly to Reno pronto.

Getting to Reno was a story in itself because I had never flown before. I rushed to an airline ticket office and said, "I want a ticket on the first plane leaving for Reno."

Unfortunately, I didn't say, "A plane that will be the first to reach Reno." I said, "The first plane *leaving* for Reno," and the idiot ticket seller took me literally. That plane turned out to be a milk run DC3 that made three stops before it even got out of New York State, and it took twenty-eight hours to get to Reno, stopping at every little flyspeck on the map between New York and Nevada.

I finally arrived at Reno and found that Joanie had met a big, rugged, wealthy oilman named Jack who could have doubled for

John Wayne. He was a husky, weather-beaten hunk in boots and a cowboy outfit. He would have made the Marlboro Man look like a wimp.

So there I was, a tenderfoot from New York, getting off the plane in my little topcoat (it was cold back east) and my little hat and my little scarf and my little pair of gloves, not to mention my pale, white, untouched-by-the-sun skin—as contrasted to the big, bronzed, brawny Westerner who had set Joanie in his sights.

She later told me, "Stan, I must admit, when I saw you get off that plane, looking like a little lost Boy Scout among all those rugged cowboy types, I thought to myself for a moment, What am I getting into?"

Well, I don't know whether it was my irresistible charm or the fact that all those oilmen and cattle ranchers looked alike, but in some inexplicable way I managed to stay in the running. But I knew I'd have to move fast. I may have been klutzy up till then, but I wasn't stupid! I wasn't going to let this fabulous female out of my sight until I had a ring or lasso or harness or something on her! By now the six weeks were up so I rushed her into a judge's office where she was granted her divorce.

But I still wasn't about to take any chances. I didn't dare let her stay single for more than a few minutes. So I told the judge we wanted to get married—*now.* He had no problem with that; it meant an extra fee for him. He simply walked us through a door into the next room. It seems he had one room for divorces and one for marriages, which was fine with me.

There was another couple in that adjoining room, also waiting to be married. They needed witnesses, as did we. So the judge said, "You two be their witnesses and they'll be your witnesses." Sounded like a plan to us.

The ceremonies took about sixty seconds each, after which we two couples became very emotional, swearing we'd always be friends and would meet every year at that same date to celebrate our marriages.

Within minutes, we had forgotten their names. It was probably mutual. We never heard from them again. How temporal is transient sentiment.

That's where and when Joan Clayton Boocock became Mrs. Stan Lee. It was December 5, 1947, just short of two weeks before Stan's twenty-fifth birthday and three weeks short of Christmas. Stan always thought she was the best birthday or Christmas present he ever got.

How did I *really* know she was the one?

Until I met Joanie I had done a lot of dating. There was one girl I liked a lot. In fact, I was thinking of proposing to her. But one night, when we were having dinner in a restaurant, a great-looking female walked by. I remember thinking, Gee, if only I were here alone, I'll bet I could meet her. At that moment I opted not to propose. I decided I'd wait to find a girl whom I wouldn't want to trade for anyone. And find her I did.

Joanie and I took the train back to New York. I'd had enough of flying for a while. Next came the biggest hurdle of all: I had to introduce my wife to my mother, who was a nice, rather old-fashioned Jewish lady. I was about to have Mom meet my new Episcopalian wife who enjoyed smoking, took an occasional drink, had been married once before, and was (gasp!) a model.

"So, Mom, this is Joanie, my wife," said I, nervously. The amazing thing was that my mother accepted Joanie right from the start. Oh, it was more than "accepted." She loved her. It gave me new respect for my mother's judgment and, as time went by, I began to realize that Joanie had a quality that made everyone love her.

It goes without saying that my father was totally taken by Joanie, too. He came to visit us every chance he had and I always suspected that it was as much to see my wife as me. Joanie knew how to keep the conversation light and cheerful and I think her presence was like a tonic to him.

As far as I'm concerned, with the exception of the birth of our daughter three years later, everything else in my life was simply anticlimactic. Joanie and I have been married over fifty years now, and with a little luck, I'm beginning to suspect that it might really last.

Stan's adjustment to married life proved to be just as quick and easy as his adjustment to civilian life had been. Strangely enough, he and Joan never went on a honeymoon. But then, Stan rarely did things in a conventional manner. As he would later tell it, there seemed no need for one. Every minute they spent together was like a honeymoon. He was eager to get back to the work he loved and Joan was equally eager to begin her new life as a married woman.

We moved into a crazy brownstone apartment on Manhattan's Ninety-sixth Street, between Fifth and Lexington Avenues. I say crazy because although one of its great features was a fantastic skylight, the skylight just happened to be in the bathroom—the biggest bathroom we'd ever seen. Unfortunately, the living room was the smallest. And it's lucky Joanie and I were compatible because the bedroom only had room for one very, very narrow bed. We used to say it was so small you had to go outside to change your mind. There was also a fireplace, which, naturally, didn't work. But it was our first apartment together and we loved it. Oh, and best of all, it had a terrace. Talk about romantic!

That was when I learned that Joanie loved to decorate. Within a few days our little inglenook was the most colorful, comfortable, eye-pleasing pad in town. We did most of our shopping for furniture and knickknacks in Greenwich Village, ate hamburgers in Prexy's on Eighth Street (not there anymore, darn it), and naturally rode the bus each way.

There's one thing I'll never forget during those early days as newlyweds, before the age of political correctness. I decided to start as I meant to finish, to declare myself master of the household right up front. So I said to Joanie, "You've got to give up modeling and any thoughts of ever again being an actress. I don't want a wife of mine to work." I expected an argument, or at least a token protest. But Joanie simply smiled sweetly and said, "Okay, honey, if that's what you want."

It was the biggest mistake of my life. That talented creature would certainly have become a star and I could have been one of the idle rich. Instead, she devoted herself to keeping house, decorating, cooking, entertaining, charming our friends, and becoming a world-class, black-belt, state-of-the-art shopper, while I keep telling myself, Stan, you've got a biiiig mouth! But I wouldn't change any of it.

When my mother died, our life changed dramatically. Joanie didn't like that change at first because, being British, she was never comfortable with change. We had been terribly happy where we were, but we now found it necessary to move to a house. The reason was Larry, my then fifteen-year-old brother, who had been living with my mother but now had to move in with us. So, it was out of the city and into a tiny house in Woodmere, on Long Island.

While I might have expected Joanie to be less than overjoyed about having my brother living with us so soon in our marriage, she took it like a trouper and couldn't have been nicer or more considerate of Larry. We did what we could to make his stay with us as pleasant as possible and he too was as considerate and easy to get along with as anyone could have wished.

But once Joanie got New York out of her mind, the house itself proved to be the most exciting development to her. She and her family had always lived in houses back in England, while I had always lived in apartments. So it took her far less time to adjust than it did me.

It was then that I became aware that a house is more than a house to Joanie. It's an ever-fascinating plaything. She played with our first house (and with every subsequent house we've owned) with the same joy and intensity that other people devote to golf or bingo. Joanie is almost never happier than when rearranging furniture, redecorating, or working in the garden. What a bonus that is for a guy who spends so much time writing to have a wife who can keep herself busy at home for hours on end.

Not to belabor the subject, but I have to mention one other thing. We all know that a woman hates to wear the same outfit to the same function twice. Well, my wife, who's the best decorator I

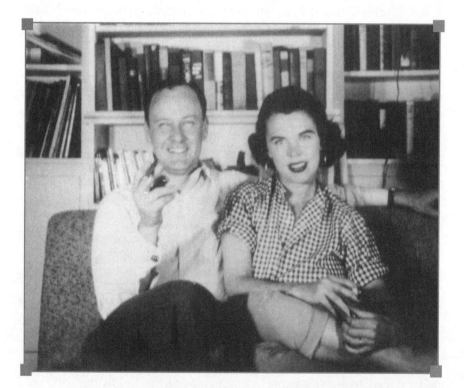

A typical suburban couple at home on Long Island.
You can tell we're both extremely camera shy.

know, sometimes feels that way about our furniture. Often, when guests were due to come to our house for a second visit, Joanie would have a great time rearranging the furniture before their arrival. It was like, "Well, they've already seen it this way. Now I'll give them something new to look at." She's always changing things around and somehow manages to improve the look each time. However, it's risky for me to get up at night and walk into another room in the dark; I never know what I'll trip over that wasn't there the day before.

Coincidentally with our move out to Long Island, I felt it was mandatory that we get a new car.

Since I missed the Buick convertible I'd had in the army, we sold our four-door sedan and bought another convertible, by coincidence also a Buick, that had once belonged to the owner of the Blue Angel, a glamorous nightclub in Manhattan named after Marlene Dietrich's famous movie. The car had a huge flying female as a radiator ornament, similar to a Rolls-Royce, and it was painted an unusual, deep, dramatic-looking shade of green. Man, how we loved that car.

After adding Larry and the convertible to our little family, we had another new arrival in the person of baby Joan Celia; the Celia taken from my mother's first name. This exquisitely awesome addition to our life was born in spite of warnings that Joanie had hormone problems and might not conceive. But conceive she did and, thanks to a necessary Caesarian, we became the proudest parents in the Western Hemisphere.

With all this going on, we moved to a larger home, an ex-carriage house in Hewlett Harbor, where we spent a couple of decades as a typical suburban family.

I wouldn't consider any other first name for our new baby girl than Joan. So we called mother "Big Joan" and baby "Little Joan." That worked for years until Little Joan became taller than Big Joan and the names sounded foolish. So Little Joan started calling herself J.C., utilizing her first initials. After a while, though, we all felt that J.C. just sounded too cold and businesslike for someone so pretty and feminine, so we decided to live with the confusion of calling them both Joanie and the devil take the hindmost.

Three years after Joanie was born we had another daughter. Had she been a boy, we had planned to call him Stan. It suddenly occurs to me that we both must have been somewhat vainglorious. At any rate, we called her Jan instead (as close as we could get to Stan), but fate had other plans for her and she died three days after she was born. It was the first, and most heartbreaking, tragedy of our lives. Both births had been Caesarians and, to compound the tragedy, the doctor told Joanie she couldn't have any more children.

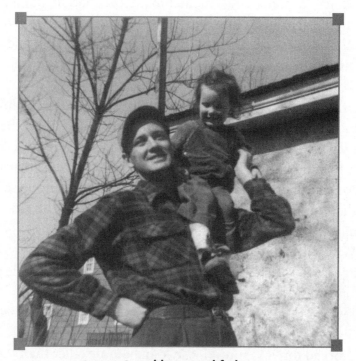

Joanie C. and her proud father—
like no one else ever had a daughter, right?

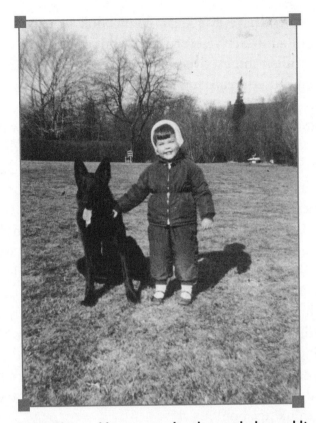

What a combo! The world's greatest daughter with the world's greatest German shepherd on the world's greatest lawn in Hewlett Harbor.

We tried to adopt another child but we tried too soon. Joanie was still too emotionally shaken up. When the agency personnel would say things like, "How can you prove you'd be a good mother?" she couldn't take it. We also had another problem. My parents were Jewish and Joan is Episcopalian, and in those days it was more difficult to adopt in a mixed marriage. Not to harp on the subject too long, we finally just gave up. Looking back, I'm not sure we made the right decision, but life goes on.

People often ask how both Joans feel about my work. While they seem happy that I've achieved some measure of success, neither of them have ever been comicbook or comic strip fans and I'm not sure they've ever really read any strips I've written. There are other things I've written that they've read and that we've discussed at great length, but comics have just never been their bag.

When we were together, Joanie and I would always talk a blue streak, but never about comics. Perhaps that's one of the things that makes for a good relationship; I can be relaxed and Joanie isn't bored listening to me talk about things in which she has no interest.

In those days I loved going out to dinner and so did she. Since we were lucky enough to have Nurse Kelly, the most wonderful nanny in the world, who looked after Little Joan while we were out, we tried to go out as often as possible. Then we'd come home and watch TV for an hour or so until I'd go into my room and write until two or three in the morning while Joanie would start rearranging furniture or read or whatever it was she did while I was working. In those days, I seemed able to write until the early hours of the morning without getting tired. Of course, today I get tired just thinking about it.

It occurs to me that I spent more time at home with Joanie than most working husbands do with their wives. Here's how that happened . . .

During the early sixties I was writing a great deal of our stories myself. I'd do my editing at the office during working hours, and then go home and write evenings and weekends. But it reached the point when there was just too much to write.

I told Joanie I was going to ask Martin Goodman to let me stay home one day a week, on Wednesdays, to be able to get all my writing done. She said he'd never agree to that. He wasn't the sort of Samaritan that would pay me a full salary for a four-day work week. But I told her I had to try. I asked. He agreed. I stayed home Wednesdays and wrote.

But once again the workload became too heavy, with more and more books being added. So, instead of Wednesdays, I next took Tuesdays and Thursdays off and worked at the office three days a week. Joanie could hardly believe it.

I guess you can anticipate the next development. I soon needed still more time to write. It ended up with me going to the office Tuesdays and Thursdays and writing at home three days a week, plus evenings and Sundays, of course.

The next logical question might be, how could I get my editing done on all those books by spending only two days a week at the office? It wasn't too hard, really, since I was doing so much of the writing myself and, if I may be totally candid, I'm my own biggest fan. Since I liked everything I wrote, there wasn't that much editing needed.

On the days when I was working at home, many of the artists who lived in the area would bring their artwork to the house for me to check. It was easier for them than waiting for one of the two days I'd be in the office and having to go all the way to Manhattan, since many of them also lived on Long Island. Of course I'd make the time to go over the artwork while they were there. We had such a backbreaking production schedule, producing dozens of titles a month, that I couldn't let any freelancer cool his heels just because I didn't take time to process his work.

So things were going along pretty smoothly for me as long as I could keep writing at a fast pace. I was well paid, by comicbook standards anyway, and even found time to squeeze in some other kinds of freelance work. I did a few newspaper strips, magazine articles, and some radio work; and that never seemed to bother Martin Goodman, probably because he felt that the extra money I earned on the outside kept me from asking for a raise too often.

The two things I didn't love about my life were the one-hour commute, each way, from Long Island to Manhattan and back again, and the feeling that I wasn't getting ahead the way I should be, the haunting feeling that I was only a moderately successful hack, waiting for some elusive big break, the chance to get out of comics and into the real world.

What I didn't understand, at that point in my life, was that comics *were* the real world for me.

Never a Dull Moment

America was the new superpower—a world role it shouldered because suddenly the globe was threatened with atomic destruction or, at least, blackmail. We were the most powerful nation in the history of mankind, but our citizens were digging holes in their backyards to save themselves from potential Russian A-bombs. Or, equally bewildering, aliens in flying saucers.

It was an edgy time and the creators of comicbooks responded appropriately. The Timely Comics operation in New York was cranking out adventures at the rate of eighty-two different comicbooks every month, all of which were the products of what became the Marvel bullpen. Under this arrangement, artists and writers crowded together, writing, drawing, talking, and working side-by-side. They would share, inspire, and enhance what each was doing, while listening to a baseball game on the radio, and they could be interrupted only by the lunchtime poker game.

By 1950, America was out of a war and getting settled again, when suddenly, it was back in a new war that wasn't a war. The politicians called it a "police action," but they weren't the ones facing the bullets. The war-themed comicbooks of the time were about those who were.

During this time, Marvel's toughest competition was Entertaining Comics (EC). Its key war-comic maven was Harvey Kurtzman, *who had once worked freelance for Stan at Timely, doing humor pages, and who would, in late 1952, develop a zany-humor comic for EC called* Mad.

EC's success naturally agitated Martin Goodman, who told Stan it was time for them to create something different. As usual, "something different" to Martin meant trying to emulate exactly what was selling well for the competition. If war comics sold well at EC, Goodman wanted to do war magazines; if horror sold well for EC, Goodman wanted to do horror. But there was one internal development for which neither Goodman, Stan, nor many others in Timely's comic operation were prepared. It was the "Cataclysmic Closet Catastrophe," which befell the Timely shop when Martin Goodman discovered there was a closet full of comicbook material, art, and scripts that had been paid for but unscheduled and unused.

How well I remember. When that happened, everything hit the fan. Here's how it came about . . .

Artists and writers are the lifeblood of the comicbook business. But there were times when we'd hit a slump and there wasn't enough work for all of them. Well, what's an editor to do? Fire them? Most had been working for us for years. I knew the various slumps always ended sooner or later; meanwhile the employees had to eat. But it was more than sheer altruism on my part. I didn't want to take the chance that some of our top people, if we let them go, would become disenchanted with comics and leave the field, because I knew we'd be needing them at some later time, and creative artists and writers don't grow on trees.

So, when a slump would hit, I kept paying our best people to continue doing strips that we really didn't need at the time, knowing we'd eventually have use for them. I simply stored the strips in a large office closet after they were done. To me it was an investment, both in people and in inventory.

When Martin one day learned of all the material I had been

accumulating for later use he took an extremely dim view of what I had done. In fact, a dim view is putting it mildly. For starters, he told me that he was running a business and not a charitable institution. Then, as he kept warming up to the subject, a light suddenly went on inside his head. Martin realized that he had an expensive bullpen being paid every week and a closet full of completed, unpublished strips. He instantly decided he didn't need both.

I suppose from a business point of view it was a rational decision, but I hated it. The bullpen was immediately disbanded. Most of the salaried creative people were let go while I was ordered to use up all the inventoried material. Martin decided that we would only work with artists and writers on a freelance basis from that day forth, not assigning any strips unless they were definitely scheduled to be used.

Those were black days for me. Not only had I worked closely with all our staff writers and artists, but I considered most of them my personal friends. I knew their families. We often went out together socially. And suddenly I was the one who had to give them the bad news, to tell them they were out of work because the decision had been made to first use up much of the inventory I had accumulated before assigning any new strips. I'm aware that it was a rational business decision, but that didn't make it any easier for me—or for the people who were let go.

At that time, Stan had an experience he would never forget. One of the artists who was due to be fired, let's call him Frank, had a new baby on the way and Stan knew how much he needed his job. So Stan did everything he could to keep him on for another six months. But after that, Stan was told he now would have to let Frank go. When Stan gave him the news, instead of being grateful for the extra six months of salary Stan had gotten for him, Frank was angry that he hadn't been fired when the other artists had been let go. He said that all the good jobs had already been taken and now he'd be too late to apply for any.

Stan had learned the hard way that you can't please everybody.

After that, we never again had the same large staff of writers and artists. With a few exceptions, most of the scripts and artwork were done by freelancers while only the production people and editors were kept on staff.

It was about that time that Martin decided to consolidate many of his different companies into one entity, which he called Atlas. I'm sure that the name change thrilled and impressed the various ex-staffers who were now tightening their belts.

As for me, I was still compelled to keep up with my own writing as if nothing had happened, and I did it from our home in Hewlett Harbor, on Long Island's south shore.

It's strange, but I was never able to write my best in the office, even if there were no disturbances. I guess I'm a creature of habit. I like being in my room, in my house, hearing Joanie moving about the place, knowing the dogs are nearby, and having all my reference books and paraphernalia close at hand. Even though I really don't like having to sit alone in a room for hours at a time, pounding on a set of keys, the home atmosphere somehow made it more bearable, and still does.

Of course, most people never understood. They'd say, "What a lucky guy. You get to stay home a few days a week." I'd try to explain that I wasn't vacationing at home, I worked harder there than I did in the office. Those scripts didn't write themselves.

Even though I yield to no man in my dedication to my job, it's a fact that I really didn't work as hard in the office as at home. After all, at the office I was the editor and art director; I told the staff what to do. It's not particularly tough to give orders and keep things rolling. I was free to move around, talk to people, make phone calls, have long business lunches. But at home I was *work-*

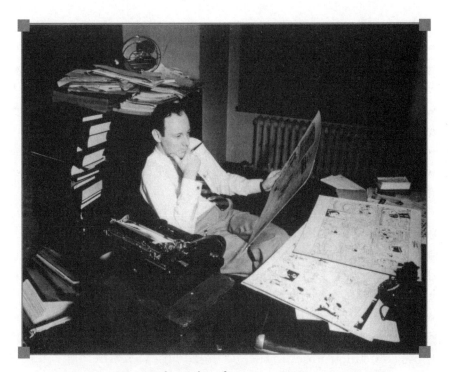

As you can see, it takes a lot of intense concentration to write
"Posty Pelican meets Silly Seal and Ziggy Pig."

ing. And I mean all day long and most of the night. After all those
years of typing I've probably got the strongest fingertips of anyone. See? Life has a way of furnishing rewards.

Living on Long Island, I couldn't wait till summertime. When
the warm weather rolled around, I no longer had to work in soli-
tary confinement in my "gloom room" as I called it. I love the sun
and I found my own peculiar way of doing my writing on the terrace outside.

The deleterious effect of sitting and typing for a long period
of time always concerned me. I was sure I'd eventually become fat
and potbellied because my work was so sedentary. Therefore, during the summer, I developed a method of writing whereby I could

do it standing up. I'd take a bridge table, put it on the terrace, and put another little table on top of that. Then I put my typewriter on top of that. As the sun started in the east, I positioned myself to face it. In a couple of hours the sun had moved westward and I would move the table, the typewriter, and myself so I could keep facing it. For most of the day I'd stand and type, continually moving so I was facing the sun and always using a lot of suntan oil, which now, in our enlightened age, we have learned was the worst thing you could do to your skin.

Joanie, in the meantime, had a lot of friends who were always coming over to our house. We didn't have a real swimming pool, so we bought one of those round, plastic ones, about fifteen feet in diameter. It was really small. Well, no way was my wife going to have that silly-looking thing sticking up in the yard, so she had somebody come to dig a hole and bury the pool. Then she put rocks around it and planted shrubbery, till it looked like one of those colorful grottoes in the old *Tarzan* movies, where the jungle lord would frolic merrily with his pet chimp. Tiny as it was, it was gorgeous. It looked like it had been born in the ground. Every time company came over, that's where they congregated, and it was right near the terrace where I was working. So they'd all be gathered around the pool talking and laughing and splashing up a storm while I'd be writing scripts and trying not to pay attention. They got so used to seeing me, it was like I wasn't there. As for me, I loved every minute of it. During those great days, writing didn't seem to be the lonely job I always felt it was.

Considering the amount of time Stan spent writing, he still managed to have time for the many close friends that were so important to Joanie and him. One couple in particular were their closest neighbors, Edith and Bob Goodkind. To this day, Stan still laughs about the fact that, although Bob was a very successful stockbroker with a seat on the New York Stock Exchange, he and Edie never seemed to have any of the simplest items in their very luxurious house. For example, their sons, Tommy and Jimmy, who were great fans of Stan's, would often ring the Lee doorbell and ask if they could borrow a hammer, or a dictionary, or a ball of string, things that one would expect any household to have at hand. Now, when Stan still kids young Jimmy, who's a successful entertainment lawyer in Los Angeles, about the fact that his was probably the only household in America that didn't have a simple screwdriver, Jimmy will sagely reply, "We never needed one as long as you were our neighbor."

The house Stan and Joan lived in, in Hewlett Harbor, was the oldest in that area. It had been a carriage house for a large estate. The Lees always bought the oldest, most affordable home in the very best area, and by the time Joanie finished fixing it up it ended up being one of the showplaces of the neighborhood.

One thing I've always been lucky about: I never seemed to develop that old bugaboo called "writer's block." Whenever I have to write something, the words always seem to come to me. They may not be the right words, they may not even be good words—hell, they might even be the wrong words—but I can't remember ever sitting and staring off into space trying in vain to think of something to write. There are so many words and thoughts available to us, it's never seemed all that difficult to grab some of them and put them to work.

On the other hand, the thought of having to write a novel and having to live with it for weeks if not months, to do all the intricate plotting and planning, that's too much like work. The idea of three hundred pages of nothing but text, when I get bored so quickly, has always been a total turn-off to me. I could never get myself to do it. One reason I can deal with writing comics is that I can write a comicbook in one sitting; start some time in the morning and by mid-afternoon it's done. Of course, I've always been too mutton-headed to realize that after finishing a book you can relax for a while and live on the royalties. In comics, you're never finished. There's always another one that has to be written.

Naturally, I always tried to make time for other things besides working, things such as spending time with Little Joanie as she was growing up, playing with our German shepherds, Blackie and Simba, and of course, going out with my favorite wife. Like so many suburban couples in those days, we went to countless parties and threw as many parties ourselves. But then, like pebbles in a shoe, little discomforts began creeping into my life.

As time went by, Stan began to feel stronger twinges of dissatisfaction with his career. Somehow, his good salary and the enjoyment of his work still didn't seem satisfying enough. He couldn't shake the nagging feeling that he just wasn't getting anywhere. The comicbook business seemed to be more and more of a dead end.

When I would suggest the possibility of quitting my job, Joanie would ask, "Why?" I'd say, "Because what I'm doing isn't leading to anything better. Nor does it qualify me to do anything else." I told her I couldn't shake one disturbing thought. What if Martin eventually went out of business or fired me? After all those years of writing comics I couldn't, for example, go to *Time* magazine and say, "I'd like a job. I used to write *Captain America.*" Nor could I go to Simon & Schuster and say, "I used to edit comics. Got anything for me?" After all, in those days comics had little or no cachet. The outside world had very little respect for the people who produced them. I didn't feel that the years I spent as a comicbook creator would impress any future employer that I might apply to. So, more and more, I began living with a nagging feeling of insecurity.

It wasn't till later, when the company gained fame as Marvel

Comics and people everywhere became aware of the popularity of our characters, that I began to feel differently about things. But in those early days, I couldn't shake that gnawing feeling of depression. I felt I was in the one business that, no matter how good I might be at it, there was no place to go from there. Neither television networks, nor movie studios, nor book publishers were reaching out to comicbook writers. At least not then.

Luckily, Joanie is far more sensible than I. She'd say to me, "Stan, you're doing well. Your comics are selling, Martin has confidence in you, you like the people you're working with, and there are no particular problems at the moment. Why not just stay with it a while longer, or at least until something better comes along?" There's no way to refute irrefutable logic. So I stayed.

Stan remembers when Mickey Spillane worked for Timely writing comicbooks. He too was good at it, but he believed he was cut out for something better. One day, Spillane gave everything up, moved to Woodstock, New York, and isolated himself in a cabin while he wrote I, the Jury. *Stan kept in touch with him for a time and thought he was a great guy—still thinks so.*

I used to think, How terrific for Mickey. I wished I could try something like that, but I couldn't have afforded to just take off like that—we had a mortgage to pay and the usual family expenses. I never quite knew how Mickey managed to do it. So, heeding Joanie's advice and not knowing what else to do anyway, I put all thoughts of quitting out of my mind and remained at what had then become Atlas Comics.

In a way, things were almost too easy for me. Anytime we needed extra money, I could always write more scripts. If Joanie wanted to buy a new wardrobe or I wanted to get a new TV or the latest camera equipment, I'd say, "Well, I'll write a couple of extra

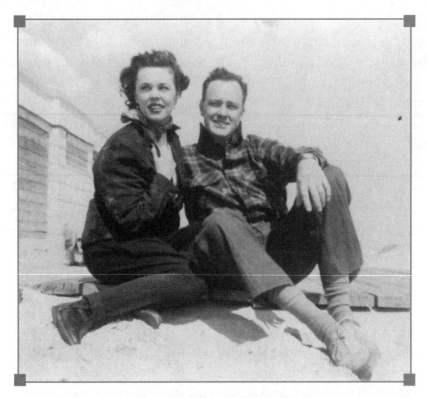

Joanie and I loved the beach.
We promised ourselves that one day we'd bring bathing suits.

stories and that'll take care of it." I guess that's one of the reasons I wrote so much. I could buy almost anything I wanted because I could pay by writing stories, but because of that, I couldn't stop writing the stories. It was like I was chasing my tail all the time. It wasn't anything that I really worried about. I'm not much of a worrier. But I could never fully shake that feeling of vague dissatisfaction.

And so Stan still fretted about where he was and where he was going. He couldn't shake the feeling that there was no security in doing comicbooks. Where would he go if the bottom fell out of the business? Who would want an ex-comicbook hack? Even worse, he suspected that he and Joan weren't saving enough money; every raise he got seemed to be sucked away in higher taxes. He felt he was going nowhere, getting older, and still writing comicbooks.

Soon, he'd have to face the fate he dreaded.

Seduction of
the Gullible

The new menace to Stan's career had narrow eyes behind bifocal glasses perched in the middle of a pinched, sour-looking face and went by the name of Dr. Frederic Wertham. A New York psychiatrist, he launched a crusade against the comicbook industry, charging that comicbooks led to violence, sexual permissiveness, and crime. His proof: Many of the disturbed and delinquent young children he saw in his practice read comicbooks, which may have been because Book-of-the-Month Club selections weren't available to them. Wertham particularly attacked superheroes, the bread and butter of Martin Goodman's comics and the daily fare that Stan created. The doctor's charge against superheroes was, "They arouse in children fantasies of sadistic joy in seeing other people punished over and over again while you remain immune. We call it the Superman complex." Shades of the Nazis and their Aryan theories! Wertham also suggested that the superheroes had sexual affairs with their teenage companions in comicbooks and that romance comicbooks were enticing young girls to turn to prostitution.

As if his diatribes weren't depressing enough, Wertham wrote a book called Seduction of the Innocent (1954), in which he blamed comics for juvenile delinquency, homosexuality, and Communism, arguing that the comicbook industry should be put out of business. For example, he said Superman's flying through the air inspired kids *to jump off buildings, and Robin's bare legs encouraged homosexuality, while voluptuous women in comics were causing young girls to stuff their bras in attempting to look more sexual. He also held that comicbooks encouraged young people to violence and crime by portraying conflict among people—a claim that could also be made about Shakespeare and the Bible.*

A lot of people bought into Wertham's ranting, which is why Stan referred to it with his own title, "Seduction of the Gullible." Nevertheless, Wertham's tirades inflamed many people across America, causing them to burn piles of comicbooks.

One of the great ironies about that period of the Wertham assault on comicbooks (and public sanity) was that a brilliant artist named Joe Maneely and I beat him to the punch. We did a story in *Suspense* #29 (April 1953) called "The Raving Maniac," in which I played me. Clever casting! In the story, I was the head man at a comicbook company when suddenly, some nutcase, raving maniac came crashing in to upbraid me about the evils of comicbooks. He said all the things that people like Wertham would later say, that comicbooks distorted and twisted young minds with tales of horror, crime, and depravity. The comicbook executive whom I portrayed lashed back with some of the usual arguments plus a new one or two. He said nobody was forced to read comicbooks or compelled to make their children read them. Nor does anyone want the government dictating what we can or cannot read or write. Finally, comicbooks are just one of many forms of imaginative escapism that we all need and enjoy. Naturally, those points were so powerful in that comicbook story that the raving maniac slunk off in utter defeat. But that was fiction. I wish we could have dismissed Dr. Frederic Wertham as easily in the months that followed.

What some people called "Wertham's War" may have been triggered by the nationally televised hearings of Senator Estes Kefauver. Like all politicians thrust into the limelight of the exciting new television medium, Kefauver seemed to be a man in search of a crusade.

The Senate began hearings into "criminal activities" in the United States on May 26, 1950, in Miami. It was in this highly charged atmosphere that Dr. Wertham appeared before a congressional panel replete with television cameras.

To me, Wertham was a fanatic, pure and simple. I used to debate with him, which was fun because I usually won—but *that* was rarely publicized. He once claimed he did a survey that demonstrated that most of the kids in reform schools were comicbook readers. So I said to him, "If you do another survey, you'll find that most of the kids who drink milk are comicbook readers. Should we ban milk?" His arguments were patently sophistic, and there I'm being charitable, but he was a psychiatrist, so people listened.

Here's an example of the degree of intelligence that Dr. Wertham brought to his crusade. Among the many types of comics we published were "funny animal" books such as *Terrytoons, Ziggy Pig, Super Rabbit,* you get the idea. Our covers were the simplest, most innocuous imaginable because they were for the youngest readers.

There was one cover in particular that incurred the good doctor's wrath. It depicted a giraffe in his cage at a zoo. The cage had a hole in the top of it through which the giraffe's neck was sticking out, allowing him to eat some apples from the apple tree that was above the cage. If anything could be more innocent or inoffensive I can't imagine what it could be.

Well, I was invited to have one of my Lee/Wertham debates at New York University at a class that discussed social issues. Dr. Wertham couldn't attend, but sent one of his acolytes to speak for him. If memory serves, his last name sounded something like Legman. Our friend Legman held up that same giraffe cover that I've just described and started ranting about the fact that every young reader certainly understood the subliminal sexual message being so blatantly exhibited in that drawing. It was hard for me to reconcile something subliminal being blatant, but who was I to contradict a follower of Freddie Wertham?

When the professor and his mystified students asked the raging crusader to explain what the hell he was talking about, he said that the giraffe's neck obviously represented the male organ and—well, you can guess the rest. Within minutes, the erudite Mr. Legman was ushered out of the classroom and ordered never to return as the professor apologized to the students and me for Legman's obscene tirade.

That's just one example of the caliber of the people who were criticizing comics, and a small glimpse into the way their muddy little minds worked.

Ironically, I had been a fan of Wertham's from long before. As a voracious reader, I remembered, when I was about fifteen, reading an earlier book he had written. It was called *Dark Legend,* and was the case history of a boy who had killed his mother. It was fascinating and must have been well-written because I remembered the book for years. I was somewhat surprised that nobody brought up *Dark Legend* as proof that psychiatrists were encouraging children to kill their mothers.

Now this same psychiatrist was attacking my field, and worse, he was getting people all riled up. I never cease to be amazed at the gullibility of human beings.

The immediate result of all that outpouring of psychiatric vitriol was that certain comicbooks stopped selling. Parents everywhere were forbidding their children to read anything that even hinted at action or adventure or any sort of gripping conflict. Publishers promptly dropped their mystery and so-called horror titles and we at Atlas shifted our emphasis to the less controversial titles such as *Patsy Walker, Nellie the Nurse, Terry the Typist,* and *Millie the Model,* along with basic science-fiction/fantasy stories, humorous teenage tales, funny animal strips, and Westerns.

Now, there has always been a degree of violence in all the

things Wertham objected to, in science fiction, and in Westerns, but the illogic of it all is that science-fiction monsters are aliens, so Wertham apparently felt it's okay to be violent against them. As for Westerns, even he didn't dare attack this core American art form. So if you wore a Stetson or a space helmet, it was okay to fight someone, but not if you had donned tights and a cape.

Naturally, as a result of Wertham's War, the market for comic-books disintegrated, with artists and writers being fired by the bar-relful. I was amazed that Martin kept me on, but then, he had to have somebody to fire all those other people for him. Again, it was indescribably difficult for me. For a second time, I was forced to lay off talented, hardworking people who were more than just fel-low employees to me.

I remember the dark day when Martin told me, "Stan, we have to let the whole staff go. I want you to fire everybody."

I said, "I can't do that!"

He replied, "You have to. I'm going to Florida on vacation and someone's got to do it."

And that was that.

While I remained in the office, I was like a human pilot light, left burning in the hope that we would reactivate our production at a future date. Martin needed someone who'd be able to get things going again when the time came.

In the weeks that followed, I tried everything I could think of to come up with a format that would sell without offending Dr. Wertham's ever-vigilant core of crusaders. I was eager to find something, anything, that would allow me to rehire as many of our ex-artists and writers as possible. Finally, there was only one thing to do.

In 1954, the comicbook publishers followed the example of the movie industry, which had solved a comparable public image problem a quarter of a century earlier by appointing a morality czar, Will Hayes, a former Postmaster General, to censor and rate all films.

Therefore, to deal with the objections of politicians, public leaders, and people such as Wertham, the comicbook industry formed the Comics Magazine Association of America (CMAA) whose subsidiary, the Comics Code Authority (CCA), was charged with the responsibility for censoring comicbooks. Despite Wertham's earlier attacks on superheroes, the CCA allowed them to be published. National Comics, which had Superman and Batman, then developed other classic heroes, while Stan brought out as many new titles in as many new genres as possible.

I think the first head of the Comics Magazine Association was a New York City magistrate named Charles Murphy. He did a good job. Every book of every publisher was sent to the Code office where each would be carefully scrutinized and commented upon. Then the Code staff would send notes such as these to the publishers, "Suggest you change this ending. Let the reader know the villain is going to jail." Or, "Please remove the line of cleavage in the heroine's V-neck dress." Or, "Change the fight scene on page two. Let the hero slap the villain instead of punching him."

Most of the changes seemed foolish and unnecessary to us, but they were easy to make and never bothered us that much. At least we were getting back in business again.

Actually, we had less trouble with the Code than most of the other publishers. We never intentionally played up sex or violence anyway and always tried to have a salutary moral message in every story. The good guys were the ones we wanted the readers to root for and to emulate, and we took pains never to glamorize the villains. Of course, we did make sure that there was plenty of action in our adventure tales, because that's what the readers always want, but any discerning reader must know that there's a world of difference between violence and action, something of which Wertham seemed to be blissfully unaware. As for sex, we drew the prettiest females we could, and yes, they had great figures. The heroes were often in love with them. Sometimes they might even kiss.

I don't think our stories would have offended a nun.

Though I must admit, there would occasionally be a proof-reader at the Code office whose diligence was greater than the job called for. I still recall one almost unbelievable incident where one of the Code's readers sent a page of artwork back to us with a complaint. Now picture this . . .

One of the Western magazines we published, called *Kid Colt, Outlaw,* contained a panel in which the cowboy hero fired a revolver. In the next panel we saw the villain looking surprised because the hero had shot his gun out of his hand. So what was the Code's objection? You'd never guess.

The panel showing the gun being fired was a drawing of the hero's hand holding the gun and squeezing the trigger. There was a puff of smoke drawn around the end of the barrel, to indicate that the gun was being fired. There was also a straight, horizontal line from the tip of the gun barrel to the edge of the panel, depicting the bullet's trajectory, although we didn't see the bullet itself or what it was hitting because that was out of the panel.

So that was the picture: the hand, the gun, the puff of smoke, and the straight line. Have you guessed why they returned the page to us, marking that panel as objectionable and needing to be redrawn?

Let's end the suspense. After phoning the Code office, I was told the panel was "Too violent." Having a normal amount of curiosity, I asked what in the name of the Lone Ranger was too violent about it. Ready? Here comes the punch line . . .

"The puff of smoke is too big!"

After nearly busting a gut to keep from laughing, I had the puff of smoke redrawn, making it a bit smaller. The panel was then accepted. The youth of America was safe once again. Don'tcha love a happy ending?

In an ironic twist years later, after the creation of Spider-Man, I got a letter from the United States Office of Health, Education, and Welfare asking if I would put an antidrug message into one of our books. While some people were bent out of shape because comicbooks were influencing the behavior of children, a branch of the United States Government wanted us to use comicbooks to influence the behavior of young people. If you read that sort of dichotomy in a comicbook you wouldn't believe it.

I decided to oblige the office of HEW by writing a Spider-Man script in which one of Spidey's friends overdoses on something that makes him so irrational that he gets the idea he can fly. I didn't know what that "something" was, but didn't feel it mattered. Every reader knew what "overdose" meant. I wasn't about to do a primer about the composition of individual drugs.

So I wrote the story as a special three-parter, one episode a month until the story line ended. There was no preaching in the copy, because that's the surest way to turn kids off. Spider-Man simply saw his friend going out of his mind because of whatever drug it was that he took. Our hero thought the kid was a jerk for taking the drug and, at the climactic moment when his friend was about to jump off a roof thinking he could fly, Spidey web-swung over to the spot and caught him in mid-air, saving him. It was action, it was exciting, and it certainly got the message across without hitting the readers over the head.

So why am I telling you this?

Because, when I submitted those three issues to the Code office, I was told they were rejected! The Code specifically prohibited any mention of drugs in any story. When I took pains to explain that ours was an *anti*drug story, my words fell on deaf ears. I told them that the United States Office of Health, Education, and Welfare—at the seat of our national government in Washington, D.C.—had specifically requested such a story.

Their answer was, "Sorry. If we make an exception with you . . . ," etc.

Well, I figured there was only one thing to do. I sent the stories to the printer without the Code's seal of approval on the cover. It was the only time we had ever done that, and I was proud of Martin Goodman for backing me up. The issues were best-sellers. We received letters of commendation from more antidrug organizations than I had known existed as well as from schools, parent groups, and religious leaders. Even the *New York Times* wrote a glowing report about the incident. But then, a funny thing happened. You know, when the *New York Times* writes something, papers throughout the country usually pick it up. So a lot of papers nationwide picked up their article, but some of them headlined it "Marvel's Drug Issue Causes a Stir," or something of that sort. If you didn't read any further, if you just read the headline, you might have gotten the idea that Marvel Comics was promoting drugs in some way. Actually, there were no repercussions. I guess everyone took the trouble to read the whole story—lucky for us.

Despite all our ups and downs, our comicbook company always managed to survive. What really saved us during most of our periods of crisis was the fact that Martin had his own distribution company and therefore didn't have to worry about getting his magazines out into the marketplace. So although the newly titled Atlas Comics was still hurting, it was surviving. Then, Martin made an executive decision that almost destroyed the company permanently.

It's a truism that you can't entertain people if you can't reach them. If the public can't find a publisher's magazines, then the publisher might just as well not exist. He can crank out all the comicbooks he wants to, but unless he can put them on display on the newsstands and in the stores, there's no way for his potential customers to find them, and if they don't find them they can't buy them. So distribution is the key to publishing.

That was where Martin was smart in having his own distribution company, a company that sold and delivered our comicbooks to the marketplace. Then, suddenly, in an inexplicable, penny-wise, pound-idiotic move, Martin gave up his own distribution company and contracted with the American News Company to distribute our books. It would save money, he explained when I asked about it, and when I said, "But we already have a good distribution company—our own," he replied, "Stan, you wouldn't understand. It has to do with finance."

Well, he was right about that. I've always eschewed the financial part of our business. So I went back to doing what I did—until one tiny problem surfaced.

Two weeks later, the American News Company, our new distributor of choice, went belly-up. They declared bankruptcy. It was like we had been the last ones to book passage on the *Titanic!*

Overnight, we didn't have a company that could get our comicbooks out to the people who wanted to buy them. Martin had dismantled our previous distribution system and had alienated all the wholesalers because they knew it would have cost them more to deal with the American News Company. Now they were determined to teach Martin a lesson, to show him the folly of antagonizing them. Try as he might, he couldn't get a distributor to agree to handle our comics.

Now, here's the worst part. With the fate of the whole company in the balance, Martin had to go hat-in-hand to our biggest competitor, National Comics, and beg them to distribute our books. They must have been licking their chops when they saw him coming through their door and naturally, they put the screws to him. Yes, they said, being wonderful, caring, sympathetic guys, they would distribute as many of our books as they could handle. Of course, they felt they could only handle about a dozen titles.

So, overnight our production had to be cut from seventy or eighty different titles a month to twelve. Overnight we went from being one of the largest comicbook publishers to one of the smallest. Imagine, it was like the Ford Motor Car Company having to sell its cars through the local General Motors dealer. You might somehow suspect that they're not apt to push their competitor's product quite as hard as they would their own.

I felt like slipping Martin a little note saying, "You were right. I don't understand. It has to do with finance."

But luck was with us. Sometime later, we were able to get another independent distributor, Curtis Circulation, to handle our line. That gave us the chance to increase the number of titles we published and to slowly make our way back to the top of the heap. But it was a slow and dicey rebuilding job, and I was the one who had to carry the editorial load. All of this, coming on the back of the horrific Wertham Comicbook War, didn't make things look too promising at the end of the fifties.

Still, we were fortunate in one respect. Since we were so eager to rebuild our line and add more and more comicbook titles while other publishers were mostly standing pat, a large number of comicbook artists and writers started returning to us because we were becoming a big market. Among them were Jack Kirby and Steve Ditko. Jack had left before but now had returned and I welcomed him happily. As for Steve, it was the first time I had met him, and when I saw samples of his artwork I felt as if I had discovered uranium. Suddenly things were really looking up again.

One of the unusual characteristics about Stan is his great preoccupation with time. He always has a clock on his desk that faces him and he always sits where he can see a clock on the wall. He attributes this time-consciousness to his early years at Timely, where as editor, he was responsible for the complex, never-ending printing schedules. If an issue missed its printing deadline, Timely still had to pay for that time at the printer, which, those days, could have been as much as $20,000. Therefore, Martin Goodman, who was footing the bill, insisted that the issues must never be late, and it was Stan's responsibility to make sure that the strips came in on time, were processed on *time, and were sent to the printer on time. Over the years the amount of comicbooks Stan handled on a monthly basis could vary from forty to a hundred, and each one was a separate scheduling nightmare.*

I love clocks. Can't live without them. In my room at home, where I do my writing, I have a clock on every side of me so that I can see what time it is wherever I look. When I'm outside I find myself looking at my wristwatch every few minutes just from force of habit, even if I'm not going anywhere. As far as appointments go, I'm probably the only one in Los Angeles who arrives exactly on time for every meeting. Much as I try, I can't force myself to be fashionably late.

I only mention the above as a little intermezzo to dispel the notion that I'm as perfectly well-adjusted as everyone thinks.

As time went by, one problem that kept gnawing at me had nothing to do with comicbook characters or plots, but rather with the plot of my own life. I was still feeling more and more frustrated and discouraged. I realized I was almost forty years old and still doing comicbooks. Was that what a grown man, husband, and father should seriously be doing? I felt I'd been too long at the fair and it was time to leave. I was finally willing to gamble that I could get a writing job of some kind, somewhere, perhaps something with a future, with a light at the end of the tunnel.

Naturally, I told Joanie how I felt, and she was totally sympathetic. She said she could understand if I felt burned out. After all, she knew how many years I'd been working at the same job, and she knew how much pressure I was constantly under to turn out script after script and make sure that the books went out on time and that the quality was always there.

She also understood that I felt somewhat like a deejay in a small town. I was sitting at the mike, getting the message out, but was anybody listening? Did anybody care?

I hoped I was a reasonably good writer. But even if I were, how would anyone know? Comicbooks were comicbooks. Nobody really thought of them as literature. They were inexpensive enter-tainment, mostly for kids, or for adults with nothing better to do. In those days nobody collected them seriously, there were no fan clubs, no comicbook conventions, no award ceremonies. They were mostly forgettable and totally disposable. I felt I was wasting my adult life and whatever little talent I might possess on a job that wasn't all that meaningful. I was just making a living, nothing more.

Up till then, when I felt that way, I'd shrug it off with "Well, I'll stay for another year or so and see how it goes."

This time I wasn't sure I could shrug it off any longer.

From Chaos to Comedy

Still not quite ready to make a clean break from Atlas Comics, but yet wanting an outlet for his creativity other than the same old comics month after month, Stan embarked on a new and different spare-time venture.

I've always enjoyed comedy, always liked reading or writing anything comedic. I don't know what first gave me the idea, but before I knew it I had decided to write and publish a humorous paperback book. Perhaps it was a long dormant desire on my part to do something on my own, something totally removed from Martin Goodman or his comicbooks.

Having very little spare time, I figured that the easiest type of book to do would be a book of photos with funny captions. I had always gotten a kick out of taking snapshots of my friends and adding unlikely dialogue balloons or irreverent captions. It was relaxing and it was fun; like doing a crossword puzzle, stimulating but the furthest thing from work.

The first and simplest thing I could think of was a book with photos of glamorous girls, the more scantily clad the better. Every man likes to look at pictures of pretty girls, and if the captions I wrote were funny enough I hoped it would be a perfect package. So I contacted a photo service and bought a whole gaggle of girlie pics. Then I spent a few evenings putting words in the mouths of the models with my own capricious captions. I love writing that sort of thing, mainly because it can be done so quickly. A sentence or two, and one page is finished. Since I was my own publisher and could pick my models, I naturally had Joanie pose for the cover. I posed her standing in the street, leaning provocatively against a lamppost, looking like a lady of the evening. The dialogue balloon I added to the photo had her saying to an unseen person next to her, "But you told me to take up a hobby."

I titled the book *Blushing Blurbs* and called my embryonic company Madison Publications, because Madison was my favorite New York avenue. When everything was finished, I made a deal with a local book distributor who agreed to take the books on a trial basis, then I quickly designed the format, sent the pages to a printer I knew and that was that. I was happy with what I had done and hoped I'd manage to sell a few copies.

The public was extremely cooperative. I had printed ten thousand copies and sold every one in a matter of a few days. The books cost me fifty cents each to produce and the cover price was one dollar, so I made fifty cents on each copy sold for a total profit of five thousand dollars.

Now I'll give you further evidence of what a great business talent I possess. I gleefully told Joanie, "Honey, we're a success. We made a five-thousand-dollar profit on the books." And here's where my embarrassing lunkheadedness comes in. I never thought to go back to press! I mean, I had the photos, I had the original plates, I had all the material. The creative part and the biggest expense was all behind me. I should have printed another ten thousand copies, and then another as long as they kept selling. But not good ol' one-shot Lee. I was just happy to have proven to myself that I could write and sell my own humor book, and it never dawned on me that I had the foundation of a new publishing business if I would have stayed with it.

No wonder Martin Goodman never made me his VP of Finance.

But, if even more proof is needed that I'm not the shrewdest guy in town, a short time later I did a similar book called *Golfers Anonymous*. I dug up a lot of photos of golfers in various poses on the links and added whatever wacky captions I could think of. Wouldja believe the same thing happened? Ten thousand copies printed. Sold out the whole ten thousand at $1.00 each. Madison Publications made another nice $5,000 profit. Considered myself a genius. Never went back to press!

But all that effort and experience wasn't wasted. It did lead to something. I enjoyed doing those books so much that I decided to do something similar for Martin. They wouldn't be books, or comicbooks, but rather typical newsstand magazines. I wouldn't own them this time, but so what? They'd be fun to do.

So I got a whole mess of photos of movie monsters and did the usual non sequitur type of gag for each photo. We called the magazine *Monster Madness* and sold the copies for a quarter each, which was a high price when you consider that our comics were only selling for a dime. The sales were so good that I followed up with *Monsters to Laugh With*. Once again, great sales. We did quite a few issues of each, which I wrote in my spare time. I loved doing them. I think they helped me get over the blues at a time when I felt my day job was becoming more and more of a dead end.

There was one other publication that I really enjoyed putting together. It started when Martin wanted something to compete with *Mad* magazine. Loving that type of humor, I came up with *SNAFU*. We did three issues, which are real collectors' items today. I wrote the first one, cover to cover, and am still proud of it. As an example of the type of screwy humor we featured, think back to the old days when there was a famous magazine called the *Saturday Evening Post*. It always featured the line "Founded by Benjamin Franklin." So, for *SNAFU*, I made up the name Irving Forbush, and

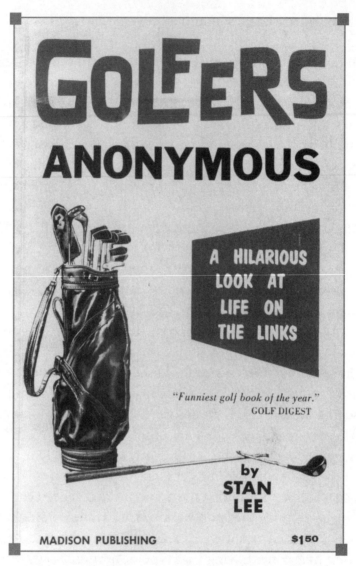

GOLFERS ANONYMOUS

A HILARIOUS LOOK AT LIFE ON THE LINKS

"Funniest golf book of the year."
GOLF DIGEST

by STAN LEE

MADISON PUBLISHING $1 50

Another one of my titanic personal publishing triumphs.
And not a superhero in sight!

on the contents page I wrote "Founded by Irving Forbush." Then, on the other side of the page, I added "Losted by Marvin Forbush." Hey, what did you expect? It only cost a quarter.

Stan produced a number of other magazines for Marvel that were neither comicbooks nor humorous. One was similar to the later People *magazine. He called it* Celebrity. *It was a very professional, well-edited newsstand magazine that is quite impressive considering that, as Stan said, he had a budget you could put on the head of a pin. It actually ran for an unprecedented thirty issues. The reason it finally was suspended had nothing to do with the magazine's quality, but rather with the fact that the company wouldn't spend the money to have it placed on racks in supermarkets. Stan eventually learned that, without such placements, no magazine of that type could ultimately be successful.*

In addition, he created other such publications as Nostalgia Illustrated, Pizzazz, *and* Film International. *At that time, the buzz around the business was that any and all of those titles could have been successful if they had received the requisite amount of financial support. Stan was generally considered to be one of the most versatile writer/editors in the field.*

But it was lucky for the publishers that he seldom got discouraged. No matter what happened, Stan simply bounced back and on to the next project.

I had good luck selling a few of my own syndicated newspaper comic strips. Once again, all of their themes were comedic. Now that I think of it, it's strange that, although I was so associated with superhero stories, any time I got a chance to do something away from comics it was always something humorous.

Some of the newspaper strips I did were *The Virtue of Vera Valiant* for the Los Angeles Times Syndicate, the story of a naive girl from Hoboken whose style I slightly borrowed from Voltaire's *Candide*. It was beautifully drawn by my good friend and comicbook great, Frank Springer. Signet Books did a two-volume paperback reprint of the series, and someday, when I get the time (which of course means never), I'm going to pitch it as a TV series.

Originally, I had an idea for a strip I called *Barney's Beat*, about a New York cop (named Barney, natch) who was hip and funny, and who interacted with all sorts of big-city types. I hoped it would be the *Doonesbury* of its day, with political and sociological gags, as well as references to what was happening in movies, sports, and music. All the humorous situations were to be centered around Barney's beat in the Big Apple and the colorful characters he encountered.

I asked Dan DeCarlo, who was one of Marvel's top humor cartoonists, a truly great guy with whom I had happily worked on *Millie the Model* and many of our other strips, if he'd draw Barney. He agreed and we brought it to Harold Anderson, who ran Publishers Syndicate at that time. Anderson liked it and bought it on the spot. I couldn't believe my luck—a sale, first crack out of the box. But things are seldom as good as they seem.

Just as Dan and I were about to get started, Anderson said he just wanted one small change. Instead of a hip, big-city cop, he wanted us to change Barney to a small-town mailman. He felt that readers of newspapers around the country, in smaller cities and rural areas, wouldn't understand the upscale, topical humor I was trying for in *Barney's Beat*. He had even picked out a name for our mailman—*Willie Lumpkin*.

Even though I'd always thought of myself as a fairly versatile writer, I'd lived in a big city all my life; bucolic humor just wasn't my thing. Still, I gave it my best shot. Danny drew my gags as well as anyone could, but apparently the world wasn't ready for a strip about a lovable, avuncular mailman making his rounds in a small town. The strip did okay, but never became the unique, talked-about hit I was hoping for. So, after about a year Danny and I simply gave it up. Sometimes mediocrity can be as disappointing as failure.

But it wasn't a total loss. The experience taught me an important lesson. I learned that a person's opinion isn't necessarily right just because he happens to have an important title or be the head of a company. I was determined never to try to create something according to someone else's lights if I didn't feel comfortable doing it.

There were a few others, like *Mrs. Lyon's Cubs*, which I did for the Register & Tribune Syndicate, a gentle strip about Cub Scouts which was drawn by Joe Maneely, one of the greatest comicbook artists I've ever worked with, whose promising career ended tragically when he died in an accident at an early age. The strip was later drawn by Al Hartley, another good friend of mine who had been one of the top illustrators of our *Patsy Walker* comics during the fifties. One of my favorite characters in the strip was a little Cub Scout I nicknamed Also who was always tagging along. He had a pet turtle that he kept on a leash. Called it his "watch turtle." As I write these imperishable words I get the feeling it doesn't sound as funny as I remember it. All I can say is, you had to be there.

The most successful humor publication I wrote and edited was also the most tragic. I saved this for last because I still find it a little difficult to talk about.

In addition to the monster photo mags I did for Atlas, I tackled a similar publication using photos of recognizable celebrities. I gave the series the name *You Don't Say* and it was an instant hit. Unlike *Monsters to Laugh With* and *Monster Madness*, which were mainly bought by young fans, this one was bought by the same readers who might buy a copy of the *New Yorker* or any other sophisticated humor publication.

The first two issues we did sold out quickly. I was tremendously enthusiastic about it, feeling I'd soon abandon the comics and just stick with *You Don't Say* because it had the potential to be an important monthly magazine. For issue number three I used a photo of President Kennedy on the cover. It depicted JFK facing the camera, making a speech with the Great Seal of the President of the United States prominently displayed on the podium in front of him. The dialogue balloon I wrote for him was, "Allow me to introduce myself." That bit of copy, accompanying that particular photo, was dynamite. We had the printer double our print order.

While the magazine was at the press, John F. Kennedy was assassinated.

There was no way we could allow that issue to go on sale. Every copy was destroyed. I was so sick at heart that I couldn't even consider continuing with *You Don't Say*. I've never done another magazine like it.

Our New Mythology

Beginning in 1961 as both editor and writer, Stan worked with artists such as Steve Ditko in creating stories every month for various Atlas Comics titles such as Journey into Mystery, Tales of Suspense, Tales to Astonish, *and* Strange Tales. *One trademark of their work was Stan's attempt to inject surprise endings à la O. Henry plus irony wherever possible. For example, in the tale "I Know the Secret of the Flying Saucer," he told the story in the first person, as if he were a Martian commanding a swarm of flying saucers invading Earth. When the saucers land, there seem to be no occupants. Only at the end does the reader discover that the Martian invaders are the sentient flying saucers themselves.*

Stan normally wrote the basic plot for each of those countless little tales and then added the finished dialogue once the stories had been illustrated. These efforts were all part of Stan's struggle to break away from the usual formulaic comicbook strips. But he was still restless, vaguely dissatisfied. More than ever he was seriously considering how he could walk away from his job at Atlas.

By the early 1960s, my urge to quit the comicbook field had become stronger than ever. The various monster stories that made up the bulk of our production at that time were beginning to pale for me, and probably for the readers, too. The titles were no longer selling the large numbers they once did. As far as I could tell, the comicbook industry was in trouble. There was nothing new coming along to pique the readers' interest. I felt we were merely doing the same type of thing, over and over again, with no hope of either greater financial rewards or creative satisfaction.

But, as so often happens, a tiny, almost unnoticed pivotal event can change the course of a person's life. This particular pivotal event was a chance golf game between Martin Goodman and Jack Liebowitz, the publisher of National Comics.

Liebowitz casually mentioned to Martin that a new series that National had introduced, *The Justice League of America,* consisting of a team of superheroes including Superman, Batman, and Wonder Woman all in one book, was selling surprisingly well. He thought it might indicate a resurgence of readers' interest in the superhero genre, especially in teams of superheroes.

That was all that the ever-alert Martin Goodman had to hear. We had pretty much abandoned all our own superhero titles at that time, but Martin knew how quickly we could spring into action when we had to.

He rushed in to see me as soon as he returned to the office.

"Stan," he said excitedly, "can you come up with a team of superheroes like the Justice League?"

Without waiting for an answer, he added, "You could use our old Human Torch and Sub-Mariner and maybe Captain America. That'll save you from having to dream up any new characters."

Martin was nothing if not an incredibly creative thinker.

Coincidentally, it was that very afternoon that I had been planning to tell him that I wanted to leave the company. I had finally decided I was getting too old to be turning out simplistic comicbooks, day after day, ad nauseam. It might have been more endurable if I could have written stories that had—even though this sounds like a contradiction in terms—more realistic fantasy. But Martin never wavered from his insistence that the strips be done the way they had always been done, with very young children in mind. He wanted the most basic plots, utilizing a vocabulary that could be understood by a child of six or seven. No words of more than two syllables if possible, no attempts at irony or satire or philosophizing. I often felt we were writing stories just one level above "See Dick and Jane. See Dick run."

Martin caught me off guard with his enthusiasm for creating a new superhero title. He was so fired up about it that I couldn't bring myself to tell him I wanted out. I decided to let it go till the next day.

That night I told Joanie of my decision. She was completely supportive, but then she added something I hadn't thought of.

"You know, Stan, if Martin wants you to create a new group of superheroes, this could be a chance for you to do it the way you've always wanted to. You could dream up plots that have more depth and substance to them, and create characters who have interesting personalities, who speak like real people."

Energized by her own enthusiasm, she paused for a second, getting her breath, then continued, "It might be fun for you to create brand-new heroes and write them in a different style, the style you've always wanted to use, one that might attract older readers as well as the young ones."

Then she said something that should have occurred to me right away, the thing that made my mind up.

"Remember, you've got nothing to lose by doing the book your way. The worst that can happen is that Martin will get mad and fire you; but you want to quit anyway, so what's the risk? At least you'll have gotten it out of your system."

That did it. My mind was made up. I'd stay with Atlas long enough to do that one new book and then see what happens.

Stan's own enthusiasm started bubbling and would bring forth a new concept and a new direction for both his company and the entire comicbook industry. It was the product of a long creative gestation that would change the world of comicbooks from that day forward.

I can still remember the mounting excitement I felt. Joanie was right. I had nothing to lose. I'd do the new title my way. If Martin didn't like it, then good-bye comics. I'd probably celebrate. But if it worked, perhaps I'd hang in there a little longer and see what developed.

The main thing was—there was no way I'd copy the book that National was doing. Sure, I'd try to put together a super team, just as they had done, but I'd make sure it was like no superhero team any readers had ever seen before.

For once I wanted to write stories that wouldn't insult the intelligence of an older reader, stories with interesting characterization, more realistic dialogue, and plots that hadn't been recycled a thousand times before. Above all, stories that wouldn't hew to all the comicbook clichés of years past.

Perhaps the most important element was, I'd try to do the kind of stories I'd actually enjoy reading myself.

But how to do it?

It took a few days of jotting down a million notes, crossing them out and jotting down a million more until I finally came up with four characters that I thought would work well together as a team. In saying "well together," I didn't just mean that their powers would complement each other. I meant that their personalities would enable me to write interesting and amusing dialogue for them. I wanted to think of them as real, living, breathing people whose personal relationships would be of interest to the readers and, equally important, to me.

I've always found that once the characters were clearly defined in my mind, the actual plotting of the story was comparatively easy; and that was the case with the Fantastic Four, as I decided to call them.

So I wrote an outline containing the basic description of the new characters and the somewhat offbeat story line and gave it to my most trusted and dependable artist, the incredibly talented Jack Kirby.

The result was issue #1 of *The Fantastic Four,* dated November 1961—and what followed was as fantastic as the title.

Traditionally, comicbook stories had emphasized overly simplistic plots. With the Fantastic Four, by contrast, the personality and character of the heroes was the focus. The story evolved on the basis of how the characters, each with a distinct personality, responded to the dilemmas and situations in which they found themselves. While Stan enjoyed writing these character-driven stories, he never dreamed they would catch on the way they did.

Nobody drew a strip like Jack Kirby. He was not only a great artist, he was also a great visual storyteller. I only had to say, "Look, Jack, here's the story I want you to tell" and he'd bring back the concept I had given him, but with the addition of countless imaginative elements of his own. I always felt he'd have made a great movie director. He knew just when to present a long shot or a close-up. He never drew a character that didn't look interesting or a pose that wasn't dramatic. In virtually every one of his panels there was something to marvel at. There have always been artists who concentrate more on producing impressive illustrations than on visually telling a story in a clear, compelling way. Jack wasn't one of them. As amazing as his artwork was, he also depicted a story so clearly that you could almost follow it without reading the words.

In the lead character of Reed Richards, one sees the marked difference in how Stan chose to portray a superhero. Instead of an invincible, muscular, all-powerful Adonis, this superhero had human failings. In spite of Richards' ability to stretch his body into any shape, he was still human enough to be a long-winded bore when explaining things to the others. Stan's approach to the obligatory female character was also different, realistic and ahead of the times. He refused to portray her as merely a girlfriend who didn't know the hero's true identity. He actually made her the fiancée of Reed Richards and a fighting member of the team. In fact, with the Fantastic Four, all the characters knew one another and their identities were also known to the public at large. In short, Stan created a superhero genre and a world as he wanted it—not as others saw it, and not necessarily as it had been done so many times before.

As far as the heroes in the FF (as we came to call the book) were concerned, it was important to me that they be totally different from each other, because I wanted enough variety to allow me to have them argue with each other and misunderstand each other every so often. Additionally, I gave each of them a different superpower, which was attributable to their exposure to cosmic rays.

The group's leader was Reed Richards, who had the ability to bend and stretch his body as though made of rubber. He would come to be known as Mr. Fantastic, as he modestly dubbed himself. As farfetched as that was, I also envisioned him as the world's greatest scientist, but so long-winded and full of himself that he could be something of a bore. He'd never explain anything in ten words if a hundred were available. His seeming pomposity often got on the other three's nerves. So, although he was a hero, he was very much like me. That is, he fell slightly short of being perfect.

Almost every superhero strip needs a female, just like almost every male needs a female. I wasn't about to try to break the mold. So enter our heroine, Sue Storm, who had gained the power to make herself invisible as well as the ability to create an invisible force field around anyone or anything. So what could be more natural than for me to call her the Invisible Girl? She was presented as an integral part of the FF's fighting team rather than as a token female who had to be rescued on every other page. She was also

Reed's fiancée, something of a departure from the usual superhero formula.

Then there was Johnny Storm. No, I hadn't lost the ability to dream up different last names. It turns out that Johnny was Sue's high-spirited younger brother. Later in the series, when Sue married Reed, Johnny and Reed would become brothers-in-law. How many other comicbook groups at that time had a relationship like that? As for his superpower, I borrowed from Carl Burgos's old-time character, the Human Torch, and gave Johnny the ability to burst into flame and fly. The main difference between the old and new Torch is that Burgos's version was an android and mine was a human teenager. But I always liked the concept and felt the time was ripe to bring it back.

Finally, I dreamed up my favorite character of the foursome, even though the long-winded, sometimes stuffy Reed Richards is probably the one who resembles me most closely. The cosmic rays had turned pilot Benjamin J. Grimm into a superstrong, ogre-like character with an irascible personality. For want of a better name I dubbed him the Thing. The Thing was perhaps the first superhero who not only wasn't handsome, he was downright grotesque. Also, he had a hair-trigger temper and was always fussing, fighting, and feuding with the Human Torch, who like nothing better than to give his mighty muscled teammate a hot foot whenever possible.

The Thing served, and still serves, two great purposes in the strip. One, as a normal man who had become a monstrous freak, he provided a sense of pathos. Fate had dealt him a tragic hand when the superpowers were handed out. Two, he also provided the strip with a constant opportunity for humor because of his bad attitude. He was continually complaining about Reed's overlong, seemingly unending explanations for every little thing that occurred. He was eternally griping about the way teenaged Johnny would show off his power whenever possible and refuse to take anything seriously. As for Sue, the Thing couldn't understand what a dreamy creature like her could see in a dull academic like Reed.

As you can see, I tried to make them like real people, with all their warts revealed. But beyond that, beneath all the bickering, I attempted to show that they genuinely cared for each other, just like any real-life family.

They were the kind of team I had been longing to write about. Heroes who were less than perfect. Heroes who didn't always get along with each other, but heroes who could be counted on when the chips were down. In an effort to maintain a realistic feeling, I even had Johnny once threaten to quit the team because he felt he should get paid for all the risks he was taking. Or was it the Thing who said that? Hard to remember after all these years. As for Reed, despite his seeming nerdiness, he was the perfect leader, level-headed, quick-thinking, and courageous. When he and Sue eventually got married, it seemed like the most natural thing of all to happen. In fact, just for fun, I had Jack Kirby draw the two of us attending the wedding.

Was this transmutation in the concept of comicbook heroes too radical to work? That was the question Stan asked himself, and, naturally, so did his colleagues and Martin Goodman. There was only one test. What did the comicbook-buying public think? The answer came quick and clear: They loved the new approach and made the new series of books an overnight smash.

Even before the sales totals were in, we knew we had a major success because of the amount of enthusiastic mail we received. After the first issue went on sale, we were swamped with fan mail and it kept growing and growing with each new issue. That was the reason I introduced a letters page in our comics and started writing my "Soapbox" column.

But no matter how appealing a hero or group of heroes may be, the stories usually end up flat and unsatisfying without the addition of one other vital element. That element may very well be the most important of all. I'm referring, of course, to the absolutely indispensable presence of a charismatic super villain. (I've never been sure whether *super villain* should be one word or two. I'll try two; it takes up more space so perhaps it'll look more important.)

I think we really lucked out with the first major super villain I cooked up for the ol' FF. I wanted someone who'd be the intellectual equal of Reed Richards and not merely a superstrong monster who commits wanton acts of destruction. He also had to be colorful looking, and there Jack Kirby created an absolute masterpiece when he designed the unforgettable image of the villain who would soon become comicdom's all-time favorite man-you-love-to-hate—the Lord of Latveria, the Master of Robotics, the man in the all-purpose armor—the unfathomable, inscrutable, and ever-irrepressible—Dr. Victor von Doom.

I thought it would be fun to make Doom the King of Latveria. (After making up the name Latveria, I've written about it so often that I swear I'm beginning to think I could find it on a map.) You see, as a king, our regal bad guy can come to America, perform his colorful acts of villainy, and then claim diplomatic immunity. Pretty cool, huh? Nor is he into everyday things like bank robberies or credit card fraud. Oh no. Doom simply wants to conquer the world.

Now here's a fascinating thought. You or I might cross a street against the traffic light and be accused of jaywalking. For that we could get a ticket. But if we were to go up to a policeman and defiantly declare, "Officer, it is my avowed intention to conquer the world," there's nothing he could do about it. You can't be ticketed for that because nowhere in any list of punishable crimes is "wanting to conquer the world" even mentioned.

See why I like ol' Doc Doom? Even though he's a true-blue baddie, I was able to have a ton of fun with him. In fact, if you won't let it go any further, I'll confess to you that villains are the most fun to write about.

Now that we had a winner on our hands, it wasn't long before Martin asked me to come up with another new superhero series in an attempt to duplicate the success of the FF. I figured I'd press my luck and try to create something that was even more offbeat.

It was May 1962. I still recall Martin's expression after he asked which new heroes I'd put in the next team. You should have seen the look on his face when I told him the next series wouldn't feature a team. There would only be one superhero. Oh, and by the way—I wanted that hero to be a monster.

He slowly turned and walked away, shaking his head. I'm sure he thought I was kidding. It's probably lucky for me that he didn't know I wasn't. I had been wracking my brain for days, looking for a different superhero type, something never seen before. I'd basically decided the new guy should be someone with superhuman strength, but I didn't want to make him a clichéd character who'd resemble Superman or even our own the Thing. I thought, wouldn't it be fun to make a superhero out of—a monster! Hey, what could be more different than that?

I probably had that thought because I've always loved the *Frankenstein* movies. To me, the monster was the good guy. We always saw that mob of idiots with torches chasing Boris Karloff, who played the monster, up and down the hills until he went berserk, remember? He never really wanted to hurt anybody. So I figured some sort of a misunderstood monster could be fun to work with. Besides, the Thing had proven that monsters could be popular. He was the member of the FF who got the most fan mail, day after day; and in *The Hunchback of Notre Dame,* didn't everyone root for Quasimodo?

Next, I thought it might give me more story flexibility if he could change back and forth, in and out of monster mode. Why couldn't a monster have a secret identity? Never done before, far as I knew. At least, not in comics. It was wildly successful when Robert Louis Stevenson did it in *Dr. Jekyll and Mr. Hyde*. I decided to have a normal man, Dr. Bruce Banner, transform into a monster and back again. You can see I have a thing for doctors. It's so easy to weave them into these semi-sci-fi plots.

Okay, now how would Doc Banner become a monster? The origin is always so important. I had already bombarded the Fantastic Four with cosmic rays, so I needed something new for our embryonic monster. Let's see, what other rays were there? It seemed to me I had heard of gamma rays somewhere. Had no idea what they really were, but that didn't matter. The name had a nice ring to it. So I found a way to zap Banner with some gamma rays and, lo, another hero was born. Now, of course, even a monster needs a name. The name is important, because you have to convey the entire essence of your concept in a word or two. I wanted a name that conjured up an intimidating, gargantuan behemoth with a plodding brain and enormous power. So I turned to two other classics, Noah Webster's dictionary and *Roget's Thesaurus*. In fact, I thought that the word "thesaurus" itself sounded pretty dramatic, sort of like some kind of dinosaur. But no, it wasn't quite right. I needed a name for this monstrous, potentially murderous, hulking brute who . . . whoa! "Hulking brute" is the exact description, and instantly I knew "hulking" was the adjective. Well, it wasn't much of a stretch to go from "hulking" to "hulk," which sounded like the perfect noun.

And so the Hulk was born, or the name was, anyway. I still needed to see the creature himself, and so I naturally turned to Jack Kirby.

Once again, Jack came through magnificently. I remember telling him, "Jack, you're going to think I'm crazy, but can you draw a good-looking monster, or at least a sympathetic-looking monster?" Even as I said it, I could hear how idiotic the words must have sounded.

But nothing fazed ol' Kirby. Instead of walking out indignantly and saying, "I've got no time for jokes, Lee," as I might have expected, he simply uttered his usual noncommittal grunt, and with a nod of his head and a puff on his cigar, he bent forward over his drawing board and later came up with a monster who was so perfect, so empathetic, that the readers took to him immediately, and today he's still one of our most popular heroes.

I've always known that superhero fans love their heroes and villains to wear costumes. I've no idea why, but it seems to be de rigueur for the genre. Well, call me unimaginative, but I couldn't for the life of me find a reason for our newest monster to outfit himself in a costume. Still, the readers would expect something colorful about him. Then it hit me. Instead of a colorful costume, I'd give him colorful skin. So I made up my mind to color his flesh gray, which I thought would look kinda spooky. Unfortunately, in our first issue the printer had trouble keeping the shade of gray consistent from page to page. On some pages his skin was light gray, on others it was dark gray, and on some it looked black. Too confusing. So for the next issue I changed his skin color to green, a color the printer had less trouble with. Although it was done on a whim, it turned out to be a fortuitous choice because it gave rise to many memorable nicknames for me to employ, such as the Jolly Green Giant, Ol' Greenskin, the Green Goliath, etc. I've always loved giving characters nicknames because it helps embed them in the readers' minds. And, to tell the truth, it makes it easier for me to remember who the characters are myself.

Needless to say (but I'll say it anyway), *The Incredible Hulk,* as we called it, was enthusiastically received by the fans, and we had another winner on our hands.

With two successes under our belt, the idea of quitting my job was slowly fading from my mind. I was too busy trying to invent still more new superheroes. I kept mulling over who the next one should be, and what kind of superpower I could give him, or her.

We now had the Hulk, who was the strongest living human on Earth, plus the Thing, who was almost as strong. I didn't want to get into a rut. I determined that my next hero would not depend on strength. I'd have to find some new, unique power instead.

Luckily, I did.

Along Came a Spider

The success of Stan's new comicbook style energized him both personally and professionally, as well as more than doubling the company's revenue, enabling him to pay a higher page rate to the writers and artists. Stan and his creative staff were now even beginning to earn critical respect, but his backbreaking schedule kept him almost too busy to notice since he was continually turning out new titles while trying to keep the old titles fresh and surprising for their readers.

Stan was a bundle of optimism after launching his new group of superheroes, the Fantastic Four and the Hulk. He started telling everyone who'd listen that The Fantastic Four *was going to be known as the best superhero comicbook ever produced. It arguably attained that exalted status by the time it reached the third issue, at which point Stan began to think his braggadocio might actually have been too modest. Therefore, on the cover of issue #3, he dared to print, in the hyperbole he so dearly loved, these imperishable words above the masthead: "The World's Greatest Comic Magazine."*

I wanted to make sure the book would be noticed and I figured a line like that would certainly get attention, if only for its flagrant pretentiousness. Anyway, even if I was a little overzealous in my enthusiasm, it would be hard for anyone to disprove my claim, since there are no hard and fast rules concerning greatness, a condition which is generally in the eye of the beholder. Besides, by issue #3 I had really fallen in love with the characters, especially the way Jack Kirby's illustrations portrayed them. It was a kick for me to write their dialogue because I felt I had come to know them so well. So, if *The Fantastic Four* wasn't the world's greatest comic magazine, it would have been hard to convince me of that. I thought it was one of the best things we had done to date and wanted the world to know it.

Inasmuch as our new little venture into the superhero genre proved to be wildly successful and its launch is considered a watershed moment in the world of comics—well, considered by me, anyway—I felt we should change the name of our company because we were no longer the mass-production, follow-the-trend, wannabes of old. We had a new style, a new image, a new fan following—damn it, we needed a new name!

Remembering that Martin's first comicbook, published before I joined the company, was called *Marvel Comics,* I felt that was the name to use. I loved the word "Marvel" because it lent itself to so many slogans and catch phrases, such as "Welcome to the Marvel Age of Comics," "Make Mine Marvel," and "Marvel Marches On." I always loved dreaming up slogans and mottos, and Marvel was the perfect name around which to build a whole public relations campaign.

I don't remember the exact date, but at some time during that early period Atlas Comics bit the dust and the Marvel Age of Comics was born!

But now we have to backtrack for a moment. We had launched an earlier title, which didn't feature superheroes, that had bombed at the newsstand. Yet, it requires careful and intense study on our part, because it was the one book that would later herald the birth of one of the world's most famous superheroes.

Come back with me to the end of 1961, just about the time we were launching *The Fantastic Four.* Steve Ditko and I were producing a title called *Amazing Fantasy* that featured all sorts of brief, far-out fantasy strips with O. Henry-type surprise endings. I loved those stories. I loved the brilliant and dramatic way that Steve illustrated them, and I never could understand why that publication didn't become one of our best-selling magazines. Its sales were disappointing in its first six issues, and so we ended it with issue #7. But then, in an effort to learn whether it might be possible to attract an older readership, I decided to resuscitate the book by adding the word "adult" to the title and called it *Amazing Adult Fantasy* #8. The readers who bought and read it were apparently enthusiastic about it, judging by the fan mail, but not enough of them bought it. Part of the problem was that superhero magazine sales were starting to soar, and *Amazing Adult Fantasy* was having an uphill battle bucking the trend.

Finally, I decided to throw in the towel. I would do one last issue and then let the book rest in peace. Just out of sentiment, I decided to revert to the original title for the final issue, so I changed *Amazing Adult Fantasy* back to *Amazing Fantasy* and felt that issue #15, slated to go on sale in August 1962, would be its swan song.

Now comes the good part.

For months I had been toying with the notion of a new superhero, one who would be more realistic than most, despite his colorful superpower. So I did what I always did in those days, I took the idea to my boss, my friend, my publisher, my cohort, Martin Goodman.

I told Martin I wanted to feature a hero who had just a touch of superstrength but his main power was that he could stick to walls and ceilings. I confessed that I had gotten the idea from watching a fly on the wall while I had been typing. (I can't remember if that was literally true or not, but I thought it would lend a little color to my pitch.) I also mentioned that our hero, whom I wanted to call Spider-Man, would be a teenager, with all the problems, hang-ups, and angst of any teenager. He'd be an orphan who lived with his aunt and uncle, a bit of a nerd, a loser in the romance department, and who constantly worried about the fact that his family had barely enough money to live on. Except for his super-power, he'd be the quintessential hard-luck kid. He'd have allergy attacks when fighting the villains, he'd be plagued by ingrown toenails, acne, hay fever, and anything else that I could dream up.

I waited for Martin's enthusiastic reaction, for a hearty pat on the back and a robust "Go to it, m'boy!" Good thing I didn't hold my breath. Martin hated it.

He took great pains to tell me that a hero cannot be a teenager; teenagers can only be sidekicks. Also, everyone knows a hero doesn't have a lot of personal problems. He informed me that I was describing a comedy character, not a hero. Heroes are too busy fighting evil to slow down the stories with personal stuff. Finally, the name Spider-Man was a disaster. Didn't I realize that people hate spiders? Martin tsk-tsk'ed a few times and went back to his Scrabble game.

Well, despite that less than exuberant reaction, I couldn't get Spider-Man out of my mind. That's when I remembered the final issue of *Amazing Fantasy,* which we were then prepping. As you can imagine, when a publisher prints the last issue of a title, knowing the book is about to be discontinued, no one much cares about what goes into that last issue.

So, just to get it out of my system, I gave Jack Kirby my Spider-Man plot and asked him to illustrate it. Jack started to draw it, but when I saw that he was making our main character, Peter Parker, a powerful-looking, handsome, self-confident typical hero type, I realized that wasn't the style I was looking for. So I took Jack off the project. He couldn't care less because he had so many other strips to draw at the time, and Spider-Man wasn't exactly our top-of-the-line character.

I then gave the assignment to Steve Ditko, whose toned-down, more subtle, highly stylized way of drawing would, I thought, be perfect for the way I envisioned Spider-Man.

And was I ever right! Steve did a totally brilliant job of bringing my new little arachnid hero to life. So we finished the strip and led off with it in the final issue of *Amazing Fantasy*. Matter of fact, I even featured Spidey, as I called him, on the cover. Then, we more or less forgot about him.

Until several months later.

In those days it took about two or three months to get the final sales figures of any publication. When those sales reports finally came in, they showed that the Spider-Man issue had been a smash success, perhaps the best-selling comicbook of the whole decade!

Scant seconds after that sales report had been distributed, Martin came rushing in to see me and, not unexpectedly, congratulated both himself and me on this fantastic new character that he was so glad that *we* had developed.

I can still hear his now-classic comment, "Stan, remember that Spider-Man idea of yours that I liked so much? Why don't we turn it into a series?"

Spider-Man went on to be one of the most successful characters in comicbook history. Although he first appeared in August 1962, it took until March 1963 for Marvel to publish him as a regular feature. Today, incidentally, copies of Amazing Fantasy #15 *sell for up to $20,000 in the collectors' market, if anyone is lucky enough to find one.*

Spider-Man's success was partially due to his several unique personality quirks and a depth of characterization that readers had never before seen in such a protagonist. For one thing, Peter Parker was the first, and may still be the only, introspective hero, one who thinks and talks to himself about his problems and his life. "Slam-bam-crash-boom" doesn't appear in every panel of a Spider-Man *strip. Rather, the reader becomes privy to the hero's inner thoughts about his troubled life. Indeed, as Les Daniels describes* Spider-Man *in his book,* Marvel: Five Fabulous Decades of the World's Greatest Comics, *"He was neurotic, compulsive, and pro-*

*foundly skeptical about the whole idea of becoming a costumed sav-
ior. The Fantastic Four argued with each other, and the Hulk and
Thor had problems with their alter egos, but Spider-Man had to
struggle with himself."*

*In the Western literary tradition, a common and classic theme is
the ordinary man suddenly endowed with superpowers that he uses
to defend and promote such virtues as honesty, love, and justice. Me-
dieval audiences watched morality plays such as* Everyman, *just as
modern audiences enjoyed works like James Thurber's* The Secret
Life of Walter Mitty—*both of which parallel the adult, classic themes
developed in Stan's new comics.*

*With Spider-Man headlining Marvel's new gallery of heroes,
sales of Marvel comicbook titles exploded from 7 million copies in
1961 to 13 million in 1962, inaugurating the Silver Age of Comics—
an era that has come to be known simply as "The Marvel Age."*

*Naturally, the old saying rang true for Stan: "Failure is an or-
phan but success has a thousand fathers." Stan didn't see anybody
standing in line to promote Spider-Man when he and Steve first created him. As a matter of fact, a lot of people who knew about Stan's
wall-crawling creation were probably snickering behind his back. But
the minute they heard the sales figures, everybody wanted a piece of
the action.*

I was surprised to learn, years later, that even Jack Kirby also
claimed a piece of the action, saying he had done a *Spider-Man*
comic years ago and that I had copied it. If it really existed, I've
never seen it and no one's ever shown it to me, and to this day, I
don't know what he was talking about.

I later learned that C. C. Beck and Joe Simon (Jack's ex-
partner) had earlier worked on a character they called the Silver
Spider, but it was an entirely different concept and the only simi-
larity was the word "Spider."

Probably the one thing that *did* influence me came from the
extensive reading I did as a kid. Among many of the so-called pulp

magazines I read was one called *The Spider*—which, of course, was nothing like *Spider-Man*—but I always felt it was a dramatic name.

The Spider of my teenage memories wore a slouch hat and, I think, a finger ring with the image of a spider. Whenever he punched a villain in the face, it would leave a mark, an impression of a spider. It was the Spider's calling card, and it sent goose pimples up and down my pre-teenage spine. More than that, I can still remember how the magazine's subtitle grabbed me. It was called *The Spider*—but after those two words was the never-to-be-forgotten phrase "Master of Men." The Spider had no superhuman powers that I can remember, as did our latter-day superheroes. He was just a man in a slouch hat fighting bad guys.

A few years ago, someone started republishing those old *Spider* stories in paperback form. I received a letter from the publisher, whose name I've forgotten, asking if I'd write some sort of testimonial for his new publication. I'm always willing to write a few lines for someone's book, so I sent a sentence or two saying it was great to see the Spider back again. But no good deed ever goes unpunished.

One day, a while back, I received a letter from Jay Kennedy, the editor-in-chief at King Features. Jay wrote that I must never use the term "the Spider" in any of the subtitles of the *Spider-Man* strip that I've been writing for King since 1977. You see, in one of the coming-next-week blurbs I wrote something like, "Next, "The Spider at Bay." Well, wouldja believe the publisher of *The Spider* pocketbooks, who had once asked me for a flattering blurb that would help him launch his series, had protested my use of the words "The Spider." I guess he felt we were violating his copyright!

Sometimes I think I must be an alien, because I'll never fully understand the human race.

Here's another tidbit of trivia to mull over. I've had a long-running, philosophical argument with Steve Ditko over whether I created Spider-Man or "we" created him. Steve feels that, although the original idea, the original story, and the original description of all the characters were mine, it would never have come to fruition without his illustrations. Well, despite my own opinion of what constitutes a character's "creation," my respect for Steve is so great, and his contribution to the strip was so important, that I'm willing to share the credit and call myself the cocreator. In fact, I'm willing to call myself cocreator of all the characters I've dreamed up, thereby sharing a grateful world's plaudits and accolades with the artists who did me so proud.

After a few years, each succeeding artist brought his own style and sensibility to the *Spider-Man* strip. The Steve Ditko version of Peter Parker looked like any average teenager, thin, a bit gawky, and somewhat awkward, which is just what I wanted when we launched the strip. I felt he had to be a kid with whom the average comicbook reader would identify—a typical high school kid. It would have been inappropriate for him to be depicted like Captain America, with bulging biceps, broad shoulders, and an incredibly handsome profile. After all, we didn't want him looking too much like me!

After a time, when Steve stopped drawing *Spider-Man*, lucky for me, Jazzy Johnny Romita was available to take over the artistic duties. Of course, he wasn't born "Jazzy Johnny." I gave nicknames to most of our staff, to make it easier for the readers to remember them and also because I felt it instilled a more friendly atmosphere. I hoped it would make our fans feel as if we and they were buddies, in a way. I'm not sure Johnny liked being called "Jazzy," so I also referred to him as Johnny "Ring-a-Ding" Romita. He probably winced at that too, but hey, I was the editor, right?

Well, Johnny had been drawing romance strips for years; gorgeous girls and glamorous guys. It must have been agony for him to change his style in order to imitate Steve Ditko's entirely different way of drawing. But he did it, and he did it beautifully. Then, slowly, subtly, little by little, ol' Ring-a-Ding started depicting the characters in *Spider-Man* in his own style, making Peter a little taller, a little handsomer, and a little more matinee idol-like, with piercing eyes, strong chin, and a heroic demeanor. He also made Peter's girlfriends look like pin-ups. It wasn't the way I had originally visualized the strip, but the change was so gradual, and the result so pleasing, that it worked. The strip had a new look and was more popular than ever. After all, our amazing arachnid was now so popular and so ingrained in the public consciousness that it was almost impossible to portray him badly.

Of course, a major element in the success of Spider-Man was the people around him, such as villains, relatives, and love interests. In keeping with Stan's new comicbook creed, all those characters were imaginative and unusual, with twists and turns almost every time you turned the page. When turning out hundreds of titles a year, it was imperative to have innovations that tantalize and hold reader interest, which is why Spider-Man *became Marvel's constant top-seller for years.*

In line with Stan's philosophy of strong, dramatic subplots, the villains whom Spider-Man faced would materialize from some of the most unexpected places in some of the most unexpected ways. Given that not only Spider-Man but also his villains often had two personalities, it was possible that a character could be a friend of Spider-Man but an enemy of Peter Parker. For example, Harry Osborn was Peter Parker's best friend, but also the son of the Green Goblin, Spider-Man's deadliest enemy; and to make it even more complicated, he later turned into the Green Goblin himself. Flash Thompson, star athlete at Peter's high school, used to bully Peter all the time and make his life miserable, yet Flash's greatest hero is Spider-Man. And, horror of horrors, even the dreaded Dr. Octopus had a relationship with—dare one say it—Spidey's aunt May!

I loved having Aunt May in our stories. As far as I know, Spider-Man was the only superhero who had an elderly, sickly aunt to worry about and care for. I felt it was always important to remember that, when working with a colorful cast of comicbook characters, they mustn't be depicted in a clichéd way. Most of the fun was coming up with surprising twists and turns. In fact, one of the best rules of thumb was, create the kind of characters that would work well in a dramatic television series.

Here's an example. One of Spidey's main villains was (and still is) Dr. Octopus, or Doc Ock as I like to call him. Yep, I even use nicknames for the villains. Oh, speaking of nicknames, I think "Spidey" is probably my all-time best. But, getting back to our example . . .

After a while, I wanted to do something different with Aunt May. So I dreamed up a plot wherein she fell in love with—guess who? Right! Doc Ock. But for an additional twist, he was somewhat smitten by her, too. He'd visit her at home, where Peter Parker was living, and neither Ock nor Aunt May knew Peter was Spider-Man. However, although Peter knew Ock was his deadliest enemy, he could do nothing about it because he didn't want to break his aunt's heart by exposing and defeating the man whom that poor old lady seemed to love. Sounds complicated but it worked and, yeah, I was kinda proud of that angle.

However, as you might expect, I'd often get mail telling me how dumb it is to have a superhero's life complicated by an old woman who should be crocheting doilies, while, at the same time, I received an equal amount of mail applauding the fact that the inclusion of a senior citizen added great realism to our series. I love to read fan mail, and never pass up an opportunity to learn what our readers have to say, but at the end of the day I have to go with my own gut feeling. So the other 50 percent of the fans won—I kept Aunt May in the series. After all, I was the one who thought of her, so how wrong could it be?

Hey, did you ever stop to think how powerful a scriptwriter is? I was able to create people, eliminate people, transform people—do anything I wanted in my own little comicbook universe.

With power such as that, it's truly incredible that I've managed to remain the same shy, humble, self-effacing person that I've always been.

Of course, Aunt May is hardly the only female in Spidey's strip. In my ceaseless effort for total realism, every superhero has to have a romantic interest, and even more than one if possible. Naturally, it's an unwritten law that they be indescribably gorgeous. Well, with Jazzy Johnny at the helm, that was a piece of cake. Early on, I gave Peter two females to complicate his life. There was the obligatory blonde—the lovely, gentle, sensitive Gwen Stacy. Then, I added Mary Jane Watson, a stunning, hip, redheaded, scintillating party animal.

Now here's the funny part. Johnny and I always planned for Peter to be in love with gorgeous Gwen and one day end up marrying her. But somehow, Mary Jane was the one who seemed to come alive on the page. She crackled with energy, excitement, sex appeal. Much as we tried, we couldn't make Gwen as appealing as MJ. In fact, a few years later, after I had stopped writing the Spidey comic-book, scriptwriter Gerry Conway actually killed Gwen off in one of the stories.

Now killing Gwen Stacy was bad enough, but here's the clincher. Sometime earlier, I had written a script in which Gwen's father, police captain George Stacy, was killed by the exceedingly evil Dr. Octopus, and, just to complicate our hero's life even further, his girlfriend Gwen thought it was Spidey who had murdered her father. So now, sometime later, we have Gwen Stacy herself being killed. It must have seemed that murderous Marvel had a grudge against the whole Stacy family.

Now it's time for me to share a creative secret with you because I know I can trust you. Whenever I write a story of any sort, I usually recite all the dialogue aloud as I'm writing it. I don't just recite it, I act it out, with all the emotion and corny emphasis that I can muster. I feel it helps me to know if my characters are speaking the right way, saying the right words. I like to hear it myself. I mean, it's got to sound natural to me, and the best way to find out is to actually speak the words. Also, I enjoy hamming it up. As any reader knows, I'm something of a frustrated actor, and this gives me a chance to let off steam, even if it's just for an appreciative audience of one—namely me.

Speaking of an audience, I still remember the reaction of my lovely wife, Joanie, after we were first married and she happened to walk by while I was typing a script. She heard me muttering, mumbling, grunting, groaning, laughing, crying, shouting, threatening, pleading, and persuading; acting every role in my own inimitable and frantic way. You can just imagine the depth of affection that woman must have for me, because she still hung around even after that.

Stan brought another innovation to comicbooks, one which enhanced the reader's grasp of the hero's subjective viewpoint—and one which tied the reader more intimately into the excitement of the story. It was—simply enough—a masterful use of the humble thought balloon.

You know, there's one advantage that comicbooks have over motion pictures. Very rarely, if ever, will a director allow his stars to talk to themselves or think out loud in a movie. But I've always felt that it was important to let our readers know what a character was thinking as often as possible. Remember how Shakespeare always had Hamlet soliloquizing throughout that famous play? Well, if it was good enough for Shakespeare—!

Now, picture Spider-Man crawling up a wall. There's no one with him, no one near him. Therefore, since he has no one to talk to, you have no dialogue. So, all you have is a costumed character moving on a wall. But by adding the thought balloons, by showing what he's actually thinking, you get inside his mind and add a whole additional dimension to the story. It gives the reader a chance to get to know the characters better, and the better you know the characters the more you care for them. So there you have the big two—Shakespeare and Spider-Man. But remember, you're sworn to secrecy. Don't go blabbing this invaluable bit of info to our competitors.

The story of Spider-Man wouldn't be complete without looking at one of Stan's favorite supporting characters, one who was there at the beginning, newspaper mogul J. Jonah Jameson.

I'll confess, I love J. Jonah Jameson, the wealthy publisher of the *Daily Bugle,* the paper to which Peter Parker sells freelance photos. Jonah is pompous, narrow-minded, bigoted, and egotistical—and those are his good qualities. He hates Spider-Man because Spidey wears a mask and operates outside the law like a vigilante. But he's an equal-opportunity hater. He has also hated Peter Parker since the strip started, lo those many decades ago, because Peter was a teenager and to Jolly Jonah all teenagers were useless, good-for-nothing, long-haired hippies. The fact that Peter had short hair cut no ice with the intractable Mr. Jameson. It also galls him that Peter is the only one who seems able to get good photos of Spider-Man to sell to the *Bugle,* and Peter steadfastly refuses to tell Jameson how he gets them.

Jonah spends a good deal of time trying to find ways to learn Spider-Man's real identity so he can expose him and cut short his vigilante career. Somehow or other, Peter/Spider-Man always ends up having the last laugh. Unlikable as he may be, I find that Jameson makes a great comedic foil for Spidey and helps to lighten up many stories.

As a counterpoint to Jameson, I created the character of Robbie Robertson, the clear-thinking, impartial, black editor of the

Daily Bugle. I tried to write the stories so that the reader got the feeling that Robbie suspected Peter might be Spider-Man, but the thoughtful, fair-minded editor would never let on that he knew, nor would he be inclined to blow the whistle on the masked web-swinger who was so truly heroic a figure.

It should be abundantly clear that I've always tried to make our characters as realistic as possible, given the fact that they were living in a world of fantasy. In fact, I tried to inject reality into that world itself. Here's how . . .

It occurred to me that since these colorful superheroes—whose destiny seemed to be in my hands—had to live somewhere, why not let them all live in the same city? That city would be New York, because that's where I lived and it was the one place I felt I could write about with a fair degree of accuracy. My next thought was, if the superheroes and their colorful cohorts all lived in the same city, it seemed reasonable to suppose that their paths would cross from time to time.

Ergo! That was the start of the Marvel Universe, a universe in which the Human Torch is apt to run into Spider-Man while chasing the Hulk down a busy street. After a while, we had so much going on in the streets of Manhattan that you couldn't tell the heroes without a scorecard. It's always baffled me why I haven't been named the honorary mayor of New York.

I just thought of something. For those of you who might be under the impression that comicbook writing is easy, let me tell you my Mario Puzo story. Mario, the famous author of *The Godfather*, once worked for Martin Goodman's men's adventure magazines. There was a time, before *The Godfather* made him wealthy, when he was short of cash and he asked if he could do a comicbook script for me. I knew what a terrific writer Mario was and was happy to give him an assignment. But here's the payoff. He came back a week later and told me he couldn't do it. He said it was too difficult. "I could write a novel in the time it would take me to figure this damn thing out," he said. Next thing anyone knew, he had written a novel—*The Godfather*. Hey, does that make me partially responsible for Mario Puzo's success?

Another innovation I'd like to think I was responsible for is the comicbook continued story. Instead of one complete story per issue, whether it was *The Fantastic Four, The Amazing Spider-Man, The Incredible Hulk, The Uncanny X-Men,* or you name it, I'd get so attached to the plots I was writing that I'd stretch out the stories to two, three, or more issues. I told myself and anybody else who'd listen that it was due to reader demand, but I suspect it might also have been because it was easier to write one plot that could last for a few months than to have to dream up a different plot every thirty days.

Spidey was not only hugely and immediately popular in America, but all around the world. Spider-Man became the best-selling superhero worldwide in Australia, the Philippines, Japan, Yugoslavia, Germany, South America, and Scandinavia, to name a few, as well as France, where he is called "L'Homme Araignée," and Italy, where he is "L'Uomo Ragno."

It was exciting to receive fan mail from all over the world as *Spider-Man* began to be sold in almost every part of the globe. I would try to learn how Spidey was referred to in different languages in different countries, but it became too hard a task. He has a different name in virtually every language in every country. I remember, sometime in the eighties, visiting Japan on behalf of Marvel and *Spider-Man* where I did a few TV interviews. When I returned to the States, I was later sent a videotape of one of the interviews and I impressed everybody with my ability to speak fluent Japanese, my voice having been dubbed, of course. The same thing happened in Italy. Thanks to dubbing, I who can speak no language but English am virtually a global linguist.

I traveled a great deal in the seventies and eighties, spreading the Marvel gospel wherever I could. Wherever I went, I was amazed at the way people in so many countries throughout the world knew about—and cared about—Marvel and its super-heroes. Whether in Poland, Spain, England, Scandinavia, or Mexico, the reaction was always the same. The minute I mentioned Marvel Comics it was as though I was among enthusiastic friends and fans, fans who would ask all sorts of questions about our superheroes and the artists and writers who created them.

In England, it might have been the late seventies or early eighties, I was a guest on a show called *Pebble Mill at One* with a host who was like the Johnny Carson of England at that time. He had written a humorous Spider-Man take-off to be performed by his entire crew, and he asked if I'd play the role of Jonah Jameson. Those of you who know me realize he didn't have to beg. We did the skit and the audience loved it. Spider-Man seemed as popular there at that time as Monty Python proved to be here in America. As for my rendition of Jonah Jameson, well, it's a pity that England had no Emmy Awards.

But lest anyone think Spidey's popularity was a sometime thing that peaked a few decades ago, in 2000, when I was in Beijing, China, one of the editors of the *People's Daily* talked to me with great enthusiasm about Spider-Man for half an hour, and I had to promise to send some autographed copies when I returned to the States.

This has nothing to do with Spidey, but speaking of China, wouldja believe I was one of the only Westerners ever to address a high-level Chinese audience in the Great Hall of the People, not to mention the fact that I've been told I'm the only American to have had two pages of original gag cartoons published in the *People's Daily?* And the title "Exalted Creator" has been bestowed upon me, although regrettably no financial remuneration accompanied that accord. I guess I'll talk more about that kinda stuff when the sequel to this valorous volume is written. Gotta leave something for the next issue.

Getting back to everyone's favorite wall-crawler, *Spider-Man*

has also long been in demand by those beacons of cultural enlight-
enment, the daily newspapers, as part of their comic strip section,
which is often one of the best-read parts of a newspaper by the
very adults who reject comicbooks as juvenile. To the sociologists
among you, there you have material for at least a couple of learned
monographs.

Speaking of the *Spider-Man* strip, I must be a glutton for pun-
ishment. After years of enduring tight deadlines while writing a
quantity of comicbooks a month, I additionally subjected myself
to introducing and writing the *Spider-Man* newspaper strip, daily
and Sunday, seven days a week, fifty-two weeks a year—and have
been doing it for more than twenty years.

Fortunately, over the years, I've devised a technique for deal-
ing with all this work, namely, get the best people possible to help.
In the case of the *Spider-Man* newspaper strip, my brother, Larry
Lieber, helps me out by doing a truly great job of drawing the
dailies that are meticulously inked by John Tartaglione, while Alex
Saviuk does a spectacular job on the pencils and that master inker,
Joe Sinnott, inks the Sunday pages with his usual flair. Heroes all.

So I guess, in the case of *Spider-Man*, things turned out pretty
much okay, considering that it all started with my watching a fly
crawling up and down the wall.

Promoter at Large

With the arrival of a new and exciting roster of superheroes, the early 1960s were turning out to be a whole new ballgame in Stan's career. Luckily, the new superheroes were becoming increasingly popular, selling well and receiving good press.

By mid-1963, when Stan saw that The Fantastic Four, The Incredible Hulk, The Amazing Spider-Man, *and others were attracting a whole coterie of new and older readers, plus an ever-growing army of fans, Stan convinced Martin Goodman to change the company name to Marvel Comics. The new name would reflect the fact that they were no longer the old, trend-following comicbook company that appealed mostly to very young kids, but were instead a new, hip, trailblazing company bringing a new dimension and a new excitement to comics, for readers of all ages.*

But nothing is ever perfect.

In the months following our successful launches, everyone in the bullpen was excited about the way we had turned the company around and about the public's enthusiastic acceptance of our new comics; everyone was congratulating me about our progress—everyone except my publisher, Martin Goodman.

After the first blush of enthusiasm, as time went by I began to notice a change in him. For some inexplicable reason, the more our sales increased, the colder his attitude toward me seemed to become. At first I thought I was imagining it, but then he'd start needling me about things, telling me in gloating tones that if he woke up one morning and decided to raise the cover price of our magazines by a few pennies, the company would make more money by that one decision than by all the work I could do in a year.

He also let me know in no uncertain terms that he paid the editors and writers of his movie magazines and so-called sophisticated men's magazines far more than he paid his comicbook staff, because he was prouder to be the publisher of the "slicks" since they were on a higher cultural plateau than his lowly comicbooks.

In fact, I started to fear that I was becoming paranoid, because I began to think he almost resented the success of our comics line. I felt it wouldn't displease him to see sales slip and have my confidence taken down a peg. To put it bluntly, I think he was beginning to perceive me as more of a competitor than an employee.

A disturbing thought came to me sometime later. I suspected he was actually resentful of the fact that people were crediting me with much of Marvel's new success. I'd been asked to do a number of radio interviews, I was the subject of various newspaper write-ups, and offers to lecture at numerous universities were starting to come in.

Incredible as it may seem, I think my millionaire employer was growing jealous of me.

Well, I kept that theory to myself. If it truly was the case, there was nothing I could do about it. If I was wrong, and I hoped I was wrong, there'd be no point in dwelling on it. I tried to convince myself that I was imagining things, that our new success was putting him under great pressure and making him busier than ever, and he probably didn't have time for the usual civilities.

Luckily, there was too much happening, too much to do, for me to dwell on Martin's attitude for long.

Every day was increasingly productive and exciting at the

bullpen as I enjoyed seeing how successful the "Marvel Method" of creating comicbooks had become.

The Marvel Method was an innovation for which Stan became known in the comicbook trade. Briefly, the method worked like this: Stan would give the artists the broad outlines of a story, describing the characters, the main plot points, and how he wanted each story to end. The manner in which the artists brought the story to life visually was left up to them. After the artwork was drawn, Stan would then write the dialogue and captions. Using this system, which almost everyone in the industry later adopted, Stan was able to write strips for a number of artists, keeping all of them busy at the same time.

Until the so-called Marvel Method, comicstrips were written somewhat like screenplays. The writers, myself included, not only provided the dialogue and captions, but also described each panel as carefully as possible for the artist. That's the way it had been done for years. But finally, I concocted a different method out of desperation.

Here's how it happened. The artists for whom I was writing scripts were all freelancers; they received no salary but were instead paid by the page. Without a script they'd have nothing to draw, and without drawing anything they wouldn't be paid. I couldn't let them lose days' pay because there was no script for them to draw.

Now picture this: I'd be writing a script for Steve Ditko when Jack Kirby would say to me, "I finished *The Fantastic Four*, Stan. I need another script to do." I couldn't stop writing Steve's script because *Spider-Man* was due at the printer under a tight deadline, but, at the same time, I couldn't leave Jack with nothing to draw. So I'd say to Jack, "Look, I haven't written your script yet, but here's the story I want to tell." Then I'd describe the plot I had in mind, mentioning what I considered to be the key points, and I'd tell him to go ahead and draw it the best way he could. I started doing the same, of course, with the rest of our artists.

Here's why the Marvel Method worked so well for us. I was lucky enough to have a staff of illustrators who were also incredibly talented visual storytellers. In addition to having Kirby and Ditko, I was the luckiest guy in the world to be working with artistic giants such as John Romita, John Buscema, Gene Colan, Gil Kane, Dick Ayers, Jim Steranko, Ross Andru, John Severin, Don Heck, Sal Buscema, Marie Severin, Herb Trimpe, Wally Wood, and so many others that I'll kick myself later on for neglecting to mention them. They were more than fabulous illustrators, they were creative innovators in the full sense of that term. None of them really needed a complete script. As long as they knew what the main concept was, they were able to lay out their panels as well (and often far better) than I could describe them.

Then, after the stories had been drawn, the artwork would be brought to me and I'd add the dialogue and the captions and suggest any art or editorial changes I thought might be necessary. As you can imagine, it's much easier to write a character's dialogue while looking at a drawing of that character's face and seeing his or her expression than it would be by looking at a blank sheet of paper in a typewriter—all this having transpired before the coming of the computer.

Also, by studying the artwork in front of me, I was often able to dream up additional bits of humor, drama, and human interest, things that might not have occurred to me when I originally concocted the basic plot.

I've always felt the Marvel Method strips were true collaborations between artist and writer in the most literal sense.

While simple in conception, the Marvel Method couldn't work with just any artists. It required people who were skilled, experienced, and possessed of an intuitive sense of how to maximize drama through vi-

sual composition. While Marvel arguably had several of the very best, by common critical consent, the leader of the pack was Jack Kirby, who Stan believed could have been a great movie director.

Jack was a master at staging a scene. Every panel he drew was clear, interesting, vivid, and exciting—he was more like a force of energy than an illustrator. The characters he designed were indelibly etched in the reader's memory. His action scenes have never been equaled. The costumes he created are as compelling today as when he first created them. His versatility was incredible. He was equally adept at superheroes, cowboys, science fiction, war, romance, horror, or ancient legends and myths—and his sense of story, his feel for drama and pacing, were superb.

When we first started working together, using the Marvel Method, I would go into great detail concerning the themes I wanted Jack to illustrate. But as time went by, as I saw how inventive he was, how skillful at plotting, I would merely give him the broadest outline of the story I had in mind and let him add the rest. I'd say something like, "In this issue I want the Sub-Mariner to kidnap Sue Storm. Her husband, Reed, has to lead the Fantastic Four under the sea in a rescue attempt. The gimmick of the story will be, Namor didn't kidnap Sue to use her as bait to capture the FF, but rather because he loves her. When Reed rescues her I'd like to show Namor's heartbreak, so that the reader actually feels sorry for an ostensible villain."

And that was about as much as I'd have to tell Jack. He would then add dozens of additional, exciting elements to the stories as he drew them.

After a while, taking their cue from Jack, all of the other artists became so skilled at expanding on a simple story premise that they could practically make up their own plots. In fact, in the years to come, Jack actually did a great deal of the plotting while I merely had to add the dialogue and captions and find a way to mold the divergent elements into a cohesive whole. (And if I ever included any phrases as stuffy and pedantic as that last one in my stories, we'd probably soon have been out of business!)

I can't talk about an artist doing his own plotting without again mentioning Steve Ditko. His story sense, too, was magnificent. He soon plotted many, many of the *Spider-Man* and *Dr. Strange* stories once those series had taken hold, and I was so busy doing a million other things that I was grateful for the time it allowed me to save. In fact, I found writing the copy for Steve's illustrations like doing a crossword puzzle, and I love doing crosswords. That is, when he'd bring me the artwork I often had no idea what it was all about. Either Steve and I had discussed the story earlier and I'd forgotten all about it, or else he drew it without first conferring with me at all, which he often did. Either way, I had the fun of trying to read the little notes he'd put in the borders, notes like "Spidey realizes he's out of web-fluid," or "Dr. Strange can't find his amulet." Sometimes I'd ignore those notes and write copy that would move the story in a slightly different direction, but I can honestly say that doing those strips with those talented guys was one of the happiest times of my life.

The excitement apparent in the pages of the new books was matched by the infectious sense of energy and enthusiasm in the Marvel offices. In this heady creative environment, Stan increased his reputation as something of a free spirit, acting out action poses and character descriptions for the staff with exaggerated gestures, jumping on tables, and leaping across the floor. For Stan, this "full-contact" approach to art directing was a way of keeping the stories lively, as well as an antidote to some of the more staid and traditional modes of artistic creation. Additionally, it kept him from getting bored.

I've always had a lot of energy and it was hard for me to sit still, even at work. I sometimes think I never really grew up, and I got a kick out of kidding around with the gang in the bullpen. Writing comics—sitting at the typewriter, hour after hour, and I'm talking about loooong hours—could get pretty tiring, so whenever I had a chance, I'd do what I could to jazz things up. I liked to feel that there was a measure of excitement in the air at the office. Sometimes I'd burst into song or play my ocarina—I was the worst player in the world, but at least it made a lot of noise and, bad as it was, it was better than my singing. Anyway, it gave the staff a chance to hurl good-natured invective at me. Come to think of it, I hope it was good-natured.

Besides writing, I always got a kick out of editing. I even edited things that weren't my business, that didn't concern me. I remember the first time I read that famous old saying, "I thought I was abused because I had no shoes, then I met a man with no feet." It seemed like a tremendously profound thought to me, but I always felt the rhythm of the sentence could be improved. Finally, I couldn't resist taking pen in hand and rewriting it thus: "I thought I was abused because I had no shoes, until I chanced to meet a person with no feet." My edited version didn't do a thing for world peace or to assuage hunger in starving nations, but I felt I had somehow made a small but meaningful contribution to the ever-burgeoning world of belles lettres. If only Aesop had taken the trouble to check things out with me first.

But, to return to the heavy stuff, on the "other side" of the Marvel organization there were "the suits"—the money, sales, and business guys. They were a decent enough group but I never really had much to do with them and I think they regarded the creative staff in the bullpen as a strange and alien breed.

I remember that the always harassed-looking suits were something of a mystery to me. They never appeared to be enjoying themselves very much. They were like grown-ups, with all the attendant responsibilities and cares of grown-ups, while the artists and writers, including me, somehow felt like perpetual kids, and must have seemed that way to those on the other side of the office. We were off doing our thing in our own little playpen, while those in the business area, the people who were shuffling paper and doing meaningful stuff, were irrevocably anchored in the real world.

While I didn't have much to do with them, I knew it was of paramount importance to be nice to the suits. If I weren't, the free-lancers might not get their checks on time, if at all. Or, if one of us needed an expense voucher paid, we might be forced to wait indefinitely for the money. Oh, the power that the business folk wielded! I also recall, in those early days, I was astonished at the way the finance department staff seemed to come and go. It's hard for me to remember many of them, because there seemed to be a continual turnover of accountants, bookkeepers, and comptrollers. After a while, they all sort of homogenized in my mind.

Even though Stan was technically on the creative side of the operation, he was extremely conscious of public relations and promotion. His staff's jobs, their work, and their artistic efforts all depended on capturing and holding a loyal army of readers, so he was constantly on the lookout for new means of establishing a rapport with Marvel's fans, building audiences by keeping in touch with them and making them feel part of the Marvel family.

I tried to do everything that the competition wasn't doing. It was especially important to me to keep a warm, friendly tone on the "Bullpen Bulletins" page and the "Letters to the Editor" pages. Here's a typical example of how I strove to distance Marvel from the others. Usually, when fans would write letters such as, "Dear Editor, I liked your story because . . . [etc.] Signed, Charles Smith," our competitors would print those letters just the way they were written. And they would reply, "Dear Charles, [etc . . .] Yours truly, The Editor."

No way would I do that! It was too cold, too off-putting. The first thing I did, even if the reader wrote, "Dear Editor," was to change the salutation when I printed it so that it read, "Hi, Stan." Then, in answering the letters, I'd never write anything like, "Dear Charles, thank you for your letter." I would change it to something cooler: "Hey, Charlie, great hearin' from ya! Hang loose, Stan." Get the difference? Charles became Charlie. "The Editor" became Stan. "Hang Loose" was substituted for "Yours Truly." Little things, perhaps, but a letter writer can be businesslike or friendly. I wanted Marvel to always be reader friendly.

I enjoyed coming up with expressions like "Hang Loose," "Face Front," and " 'Nuff Said." " 'Nuff Said" was a particular favorite of mine. It seemed so applicable in so many cases. It wasn't long before the fans soon latched onto those little catchwords and began tossing them back to us in their letters. The only problem was, the competition started using them, too. While they say imitation is the sincerest form of flattery, I wasn't flattered or amused. I was determined to come up with an expression that no one would or could copy.

That's when I started signing everything I could with the word "Excelsior," an Old English word meaning "Upward and Onward to Greater Glory!" I figured none of our competitors would know what it meant and even if they did, they wouldn't know how to spell it. Luckily, no one else has used "Excelsior!" yet. Let's hope this book won't give them any ideas.

It's funny the way people remember those expressions. I haven't used " 'Nuff Said" for many years, yet every so often when I get a letter from a fan he'll write " 'Nuff Said" over the signature. Too bad I wasn't able to copyright that years ago.

Besides answering letters, I felt I wanted to be able to talk directly to the readers, just the way a fella would talk to a friend. So I initiated a column called "Stan's Soapbox," in which I discussed anything on my mind, mainly for the purpose of eliciting responses from the readers. I would just write whatever came into my head, trying to avoid any sales pitches; it was just me communicating with them. I'd write little messages like, "Hey, I hope you enjoyed this month's *Hulk*. Didja know it was drawn by Herb Trimpe, whose skin seems to be turning green the more he draws our jolly green giant?" Or, "Did you read that last issue of so and so? Wouldja believe I only had ten minutes to dream up the plot? But luckily Jack Kirby saved me. Now it reads like it took at least fifteen minutes, right?"

Basically, I wanted to give our fans personal stuff, make them feel they were part of Marvel, make them feel as though they were on a first-name basis with the whole screwy staff. In a way, I wanted it to be as though they were getting a personal letter from a friend who was away at camp.

I even wrote lyrics commemorating major holidays, lyrics which could be sung to the tune of "Yankee Doodle" and other popular refrains and which were takeoffs on various superheroes and villains. Sure, a lot of the stuff was corny, and the readers didn't hesitate to tell me so, but the important thing is—they read them, they noted them, and they replied to them. We had a real relationship going. I've always felt that the good ol' "Soapbox" was one of the best public relations concepts in comics, or anywhere else for that matter. I can't remember how many years I wrote that column, but even now, hardly a day goes by when someone I meet doesn't wistfully refer to it.

Another thing I enjoyed doing in the "Soapbox" was stating company policy for our readers. Okay, so I made up the policy without asking anyone, which made it Stan Lee policy, I guess. But I thought of it as a company policy, and nobody ever argued with it. Maybe that was because the staff never read it, who knows? I remember one column, a favorite of mine, in which I told the fans that Marvel would never try to proselytize; we would never try to present any particular political point of view or push any religious belief in any of our stories. The only credo we espoused was "Do Unto Others as You Would Have Them Do Unto You." Good guys and bad guys were always fighting in our fantastic little fables, but in real life our message was, "Be good to each other." Heavy stuff for a bunch of comicbooks, perhaps, but I worded the messages lightly while including plenty of tongue-in-cheek references, and I'm happy to report that the fans seemed to love 'em.

Of course, the more I editorialized, the more letters I received asking how I felt about things, and I mean anything and everything. One letter might ask, "How do you feel about race relations in this country?" Another, "Do you think the Hulk could beat Thor in a fair fight?" or "Do you think kids are really influenced by movies, TV, and comics?" One of my favorites was "What do you wanna be when you grow up?"

Oh yes, there was a growing bond between our readers and us, and nothing could have made me happier.

Another thing that I believe helped to strengthen that bond was the matter of honesty. I respect people who are honest and I've always tried to be honest with our readers. Getting back to fan letters, very often on the letters page of a competitor's mag you might have found this type of letter: "I didn't like such and such a story." Inevitably, the editor's reply would be something like, "Well, you just didn't understand it. The point of that story was . . . blah blah blah. Reread it and you may change your mind." But that's not the kind of answer they'd get from mighty Marvel! I enjoyed writing this type of reply: "Know something? You're right. It wasn't one of our best yarns. Pretty perceptive of you to notice but, hey, we can't hit a homer every time. Here's hoping the next'll be better—and thanks for taking the time to set us straight."

Fans loved that type of response. They felt we were really talking to them, leveling with them. In fact, I'll never forget one of my favorite incidents, which will illuminate this most profound point. I don't remember what book it was, it might have been *The Avengers,* or *Iron Man,* or—but whichever it was, in that particular issue I had written one of the few stories that I really didn't much care for myself. There wasn't time to fix it up because of a tight deadline. On the cover I wrote something like, "Look, this may not be one of the best stories we've ever done, but we've given you enough good ones so that you owe it to us to buy this lemon anyway."

Well, wouldja believe that issue was one of our best-selling books that month! I got a ton of fan mail that said things like, "You guys are the greatest. Nobody else would have been that honest— and, y'know what, the story wasn't all that bad!"

Ah yes, those were the days.

Besides his role as Marvel's head writer, Stan was also editor-in-chief and art director. In his position as Marvel's creative head, Stan never stopped looking for new, inventive ways to draw in readers.

Since we were lucky enough to have a plethora of fans, it seemed to me that we owed it to them (and to us) to start our own fan club. What better way to establish a bond between our readers and us?

Naturally, I wanted to make it unusual, as different from other fan clubs as possible. As with everything Marvel, I felt it should have a lighthearted, tongue-in-cheek feeling to it. Even the name should be slightly outrageous. I wracked my brain for days until I came up with a gimmick. In January 1965, I announced on the "Bullpen Bulletins" page that Marvel, out of the kindness of its benevolent heart, was going to go to the tremendous expense and trouble of providing a club for its oh-so-deserving fans. But first they must prove worthy. First, they must guess the name of the club. We would only furnish a hint. It was the only club I know of that began as a contest.

The hint we provided were the initials MMMS. We offered prizes to anyone who could figure out what MMMS stood for. We kept the contest going for months, providing little clues along the way, until the big day dawned when we announced the name everyone had been waiting for. It was—the Merry Marvel Marching Society.

We made a big deal of it. I referred to our club members as Mighty Marvel's Merry Marchers. We kidded around with the slogan, "We don't know where we're marching, but we're on the way!" Next, I didn't just want to send out a membership card, or a corny decoder ring or whatever. I realized that most of our readers felt they knew the members of the bullpen because I was always writing about them. So, in a moment of inspiration, I marched the whole gang out of the office one day to a recording studio about five blocks away. In those days, you could press a very cheap vinyl record for less than a penny each. Since it was so affordable, we made a record for our fans, ad-libbing the whole thing.

Jack "King" Kirby and I feigned an argument in front of the mike with brilliant dialogue, like—Jack: "What are we doing here anyway?" Stan: "Making fools of ourselves," while our demon letterer, "Adorable Artie" Simek, insisted upon playing his off-key harmonica, and production manager "Jolly Solly" Brodsky pleaded for us to cut the nonsense short because we had deadlines back at the office. My one-in-a-million secretary/assistant, "Fabulous Flo" Steinberg, begged us to restore some sanity to the whole affair, and on and on. Our wacky little record, which played for about five minutes, was one of the many offbeat things we sent to our Merry Marchers. Nobody had ever gotten anything like that before, where they actually heard the voices of the people whose stories they had been reading. It's a wonder they didn't cancel their subscriptions on the spot! But they didn't—they loved it and it was oh so typically Marvel!

We also sent the MMMSers a little pad that had drawings of all our characters running down the margin. It was for them to write notes on when they went to meetings at the Pentagon or the White House. Since our beneficence knew no limit, they additionally received a membership card that entitled the bearer to all the privileges of a Merry Marvel Marching Society member. In other words, the worthless though beautifully decorated card entitled them to absolutely nothing, and the great part about it was that they knew it and got a real big kick out of it. We even had a large membership pin with pictures of all our main heroes on it and the initials MMMS prominently displayed in the center. I still meet men today, old enough for Social Security, who say, "I still have my Merry Marvel Marching Society membership card and I wouldn't part with it for anything." Kinda gives me a lump in my throat.

Typical of the playfulness and imagination that entered into Stan's daily work was the "No Prize" award. Readers who could locate a typographical or other error in a Marvel comic were invited to write in and inform Marvel of those grievous errors. For each such error-spotting, Stan would mail back an empty envelope marked "CON-GRATULATIONS! This envelope contains a genuine Marvel Comics NO-PRIZE, which you have just won!" Over the years, the now famous No-Prize has become one of the most sought-after items by typical Marvel readers as well as members of the MMMS.

Another innovative idea of Stan's, which is still fondly remembered today by a host of longtime readers, was the use of humorous credits. He was not only the first to credit the writer, penciller, inker, letterer, and editor of each story, but he took pains to do it humorously, writing each and every credit himself. An example of the type of credits that totally captivated the fans was: "Written with Passion by Stan Lee. Drawn with Pride by Jack Kirby. Inked with Perfection by Joe Sinnott. And Lettered with a Scratchy Pen by Artie Simek." Every set of credits in every issue was different, unique, and chuckle-inducing, and every one was written by Stan.

Out of those credits came another trend that was exclusively identified with Marvel and Stan. As Stan has said, he enjoyed giving all the artists and writers nicknames. You've already seen "Jazzy" Johnny Romita's appellation, but there was also "Genial" Gene

Colan, "Darlin' " Dick Ayers, Gil "Sugar" Kane, "Rascally" Roy Thomas, "Big John" Buscema, "Titanic" Tom DeFalco, "Jolly" Jack Kirby (which Stan later changed to Jack "King" Kirby), "Merry" Marty Goodman (even the publisher wasn't exempt), "Adorable" Artie Simek, "Sturdy" Stevey Ditko, "Dashin' " Don Heck—well, you get the idea. Whether or not the names caught on, and many did, it was a remarkably clever device to establish recognition on the part of the fans and even more, to make them feel a kinship with their bullpen buddies, as Stan called them.

Getting back to the No-Prize, there was a second idea behind that little gimmick, as I took great pains to explain in my "Soapbox" column. I knew our fans got a kick out of contests, but every contest has a winner, or perhaps a few winners, and all the rest are losers. Well, I steadfastly declared that we, thy bullpen buddies, would never allow any loyal Marvelite to be a loser. Therefore, instead of giving out a handful of prizes to a lucky few, whenever we had a contest everyone would be awarded a prestigious No-Prize. Admittedly, it was a batty idea, but it was so typical of Marvel that our fans really dug it.

These days, every so often I go to a business meeting and one of the people present takes out a tattered old No-Prize envelope he had received years ago and asks me to sign it. You can't buy moments like that.

Years later, I had to reluctantly disband the MMMS because Martin Goodman decided it was too expensive for the company to service. He said it just cost too much money to send out all that stuff. "But it's great public relations," I argued. He couldn't see it. Public relations was too intangible a concept to him. He was the boss, so bye-bye MMMS.

A few years later—it must have been when Martin wasn't looking—I formed another such club because I instinctively knew such projects were terrific ways to ensure a reader's loyalty. Still wanting to make it unusual and somewhat off the wall, I called it

"FOOM," which stood for "Friends of ol' Marvel." It was the same type of nutty, irreverent club and it was rather successful in that we quickly gained thousands of members.

But, alas, this part of the story has no happier ending than the MMMS saga. Eventually, I had to drop FOOM, too. The number crunchers at Marvel saw no reason to continue to finance it since, though it wasn't losing money, it wasn't a profit center. They had their own formula for estimating money spent, money brought in, and percentage of profit. Alas, they had no way to calculate the value of inculcating good will on behalf of the fans.

It's a shame. I always felt that Marvel could have and should have one day rivaled Disney if only those who controlled the purse strings had understood the value of promotion and public relations. We had what every company dreams of having, a fervent, fanatical fan following all over the country and throughout the world. Yet, nobody in the executive suites knew what to do with that invaluable resource except just keep publishing the books and hope they'd sell. They didn't seem to understand the value of having a great fan base. They didn't seem to realize it was necessary to nurture those fans, to keep their loyalty and enlist their support. They never seemed to be aware how vital it was to maintain contact with those who cared about us, because fans can be the most elusive, ephemeral group in the world.

Alas, the suits just didn't get it.

Our Expanding Universe

As the 1960s continued, Stan, working with his top artists, went on to create still more superheroes with human frailties and hang-ups. Some were even more than merely human, such as the Norse god Thor, one of Marvel's first major creations after Spider-Man.

But no one can describe the creation of these characters better than Stan himself.

You know that old saying about how to sculpt an elephant—you simply take a big sculpting stone and chip away everything that isn't an elephant. What you have left is an elephant. Well, that pretty much describes the simplest way to dream up a new super-hero—you chip away at everything that's already been done, and what you have left is, hopefully, something new in the way of su-perheroes.

I had already given birth to the Fantastic Four, the Hulk, and Spider-Man. Next, I wanted to come up with something to-tally different. I thought it would be fun to invent someone as powerful as, or perhaps even more powerful than, the Incredible Hulk. But how do you make someone stronger than the strongest human?

It finally came to me; don't make him human—make him a god.

That notion intrigued me. I certainly had enough gods to choose from. There were Roman gods, Greek gods, and Norse gods, just to name a few. Mulling it over, I decided readers were already pretty familiar with the Greek and Roman gods. It might be more fun to delve into the old Norse legends, and fun was always the name of the game. Besides, I pictured the Norse gods looking like Vikings of old, with the flowing beards, horned helmets, and battle clubs. I liked the imagery.

One of our established titles, *Journey into Mystery*, needed a shot in the arm, so I picked Thor, the Norse God of Thunder, to headline the book. After writing an outline depicting the story and the characters I had in mind, I asked my brother, Larry, to write the script because I didn't have time. Always dependable, Larry did a great job on it and it was only natural for me to assign the penciling to Jack Kirby, who drew it as though he had spent his whole life in Asgard, the home of the gods.

After writing only the plots for the next dozen or so stories while Larry did a splendid scripting job, I then started doing the complete scripts myself because I liked the character so much. That freed Larry up to write and draw his favorite Westerns.

One thing I have to mention—Larry Lieber is one of the unsung heroes of comicdom. A terrific writer, layout man, and artist, he does his work quietly, efficiently, and dependably. He's written and drawn almost every type of strip in his career and done them all well. I sometimes feel, in an effort to be extremely fair, I've bent over backward not to favor him over any other artists or writers because he's my brother. Thinking back about it, I feel I've done him a disservice. So I just wanna say right here and now, in print for all to see, that my brother Larry Lieber is one terrific writer and artist and even more important, one helluva great guy.

Now, we return to Asgard. We later took Thor out of *Journey into Mystery* and gave him his own book, and that was when I started having him speak in a pseudo-biblical/Shakespearean manner. I used to hope the Bard wasn't turning over in his grave.

One instructional footnote: I wanted Thor to be able to fly, like a Thunder God should, but unlike with Superman, who seems to have no visible means of propulsion, I wanted a credible explanation for his ability to soar through the heavens. I like things that appear to be grounded in science, such as the Fantastic Four having gained their powers from cosmic rays or the Hulk being whumped by gamma rays, even though I wouldn't recognize a cosmic or gamma ray if they lived next door.

So, in my never-ending quest for scientific accuracy, I had Thor keep his magic hammer attached to his wrist by a leather thong. When he wanted to fly, he'd whirl the hammer over his head faster than a propeller and then, when he released his grip on it, it would go flying off into the heavens—and, since his wrist was attached by the thong, the hammer would carry our hero off with it. To this day I don't know why NASA has never invited me to join their scientific team.

With Thor soaring off to Asgard, I was again faced with the problem of coming up with a new and different hero. We already had a flaming, flying teenager; an invisible girl; a man who could stretch his body; a green-skinned monster; a wall-crawling, web-shooting human arachnid; and a Norse god. What could be possibly different? Suddenly it hit me.

How about a hero who could shrink himself down to the size of Tom Thumb? Such a character might be a hit or a bomb, but one thing was for sure, it would be new and different. That made it good enough for me, and so once again Jack Kirby took up the penciling cudgels and Ant Man was born. Believe it or not, I even arranged for him to be able to communicate with insects. Then, because every hero needs a girlfriend, I found a way to have our heroine shrink down to the size of a wasp, and in a stroke of sheer inspiration, I called her—the Wasp!

Many months later, I gave Ant Man the additional ability to grow larger than normal and dubbed him Giant Man. So we ended up with a two-for-the-price-of-one hero. Nothing was too good for our grateful readers.

Drunk with power at that point, I was eager to keep going, to see how many more oddball heroes I could dream up. It was the spring of 1963 and teenagers were into civil rights and peace. They despised what they called the military/industrial complex and, with the Korean War behind us, most kids had no use for industrialists or those who made huge profits selling arms and armaments.

I don't know what got into me, but I thought it would be fun to create a character who would buck the trend.

As usual, I first discussed the idea with Martin Goodman. I remember saying something like, "You know what would be fun? Let's create a hero who wouldn't have a chance to be a success right now and let's find a way to make him popular. We'll feature a tycoon who invents and manufactures weapons and munitions and sells them to our military. He'll be a billionaire industrialist, the quintessential capitalist, and I'll try to find a way to make our readers like him."

As expected, Martin said, "You're crazy."

But he didn't say no. By then, almost anything we did seemed to sell. So, working with my old friend, artist Don Heck, I modeled Iron Man after Howard Hughes, who had designed, built, and flown his own plane and had been a billionaire industrialist inventor. In the course of the story I arranged for our hero, whom I called Tony Stark, to be captured by the enemy on a battlefield while observing the efficiency of one of his weapons. The enemy was about to torture him for the secrets of his weaponry. The only way he could earn his freedom was to create a weapon for them. They gave him the material, but he used it to fashion an iron suit for himself instead, thus becoming Iron Man.

Since I always tried to give our characters an Achilles heel of some sort, I gifted Iron Man with a piece of shrapnel that was lodged near his heart. It was inoperable and he'd never know when it might move the slightest bit and kill him.

Due to his injury, he always had to either wear the iron armor, or an iron chest plate he had fashioned for himself, to keep his heart beating. If that explanation doesn't sound medically correct, hey, he's a comicbook hero and I'm not a cardiologist.

Of course, nobody knew that Iron Man was really Tony Stark, the billionaire industrialist. He pretended to the world that Iron Man was a robot whom Stark had created as a bodyguard. Lucky for me as the writer, nobody ever seemed to notice that Stark and his bodyguard were never ever seen together.

Next, I got a kick out of creating possibly the first ethnic comicbook. This one, too, originated after a discussion I'd had with Martin Goodman.

At the time, Martin was wondering out loud why our comics were selling so well. He thought it might have been because they had such great titles. Even though I had been the title-maker-upper, I disagreed. By then, I felt secure enough to do that from time to time. I told him I felt we were succeeding because, unlike with most other comics, we were concentrating on characterization and realistic dialogue, which helped make the fantasy angles seem more believable. Also, I had always tried to inject elements of humor, humor that comes out of character and situation rather than simple gags. I referred to our entire approach as the Marvel Style. I told him it was that style that made the difference.

Martin replied, "That's too subtle, Stan. Kids don't appreciate that. You know what I think? I think they're just good titles, that's what. *Spider-Man, The Incredible Hulk, Iron Man;* they're great names."

I knew they were, but that wasn't the point. That's when I decided to bet that I could prove he was wrong. Remember, it was the sixties and readers were sick of war and anything that had to do with war. So, I said, "I'll do a war book with the worst title I can come up with, but if it's done in the Marvel style, I'll bet it'll sell."

He said, "Not a chance. Once and for all, this'll prove you're wrong, Stan. Go ahead and try it; you'll see."

Well, it wasn't easy to come up with the worst name possible, but I tried. I wracked my weary little brain hour after hour until I finally zeroed in on the most unlikely title I could think of—*Sgt. Fury and His Howling Commandos.*

The fact that it was a war theme alone should have been its death knell, but the title was admittedly far too long and much too cumbersome. We could barely squeeze it in on the cover masthead. Then, to make my task even tougher, I gave our hero, Sgt. Nick Fury, the most ethnically mixed platoon I could dream up. It consisted of Jewish Izzy Cohen, Italian Dino Manelli, Irish Dum-Dum Dugan, Gabriel Jones, a black man—well, you get the idea. There was even a gay platoon member named Percival Pinkerton. People kept telling me it wouldn't sell in the South, it wouldn't sell in small towns, in the big cities, anywhere. Not only Martin, but everyone, felt there were three strikes against it.

So there it was, a comicbook with a terrible title, starring a platoon made up of various minorities—something for every bigot to dislike—and featuring nothing but World War II stories that everyone told me "weren't relevant to today's readers."

But it had one great asset going for it, an asset named Jack Kirby, who illustrated my script.

Bottom line—it became an almost instant best-seller. We published it for years, and when I myself got tired of all those war stories, we dropped it. But, due to reader demand, we had to reprint the old issues for another few years, and the reprint copies sold almost as well as the original ones.

In fact, Sgt. Fury was so popular that we featured him years later in a new series that I cooked up called *Nick Fury, Agent of S.H.I.E.L.D.*, also drawn by the ubiquitous Jack Kirby. S.H.I.E.L.D. was a covert military group wherein I magnanimously promoted Sgt. Fury to Colonel after all those years. Fury and S.H.I.E.L.D. are still around, fighting the bad guys and giving proof to the validity of the Marvel Style.

And if you promise not to let this information fall into enemy hands, I'll let you in on a little secret. S.H.I.E.L.D. stood for "Supreme Headquarters International Espionage Law-Enforcement Division." When I made up titles I didn't kid around!

In July of 1963 I gifted the world with another favorite of mine, *Dr. Strange*. Although when I really think about it, they were all my favorites.

Dr. Strange started out as a brilliant, world-famous surgeon, but one who was interested only in money and self-aggrandizement. Not a very nice guy. Through an accident, he injured his hands and was no longer able to perform surgery. He tried everything to regain use of his hands, but to no avail. Finally, in far-off Tibet, an aged mystic whom I called the Ancient One cured him in some enchanted manner and taught him magic, making him the Ancient One's disciple.

So now, the once selfish, self-centered Stephen Strange is transformed into the Master of the Mystic Arts and spends his life fighting the supernatural forces of evil wherever they may be.

Dr. Strange owed much of his popularity to Steve Ditko, who illustrated him in the most incredibly dramatic and magical style. When we'd have the good doctor entering another dimension, Steve drew that dimension in such a way that you could believe it really existed. If any strip ever owed its flavor and individuality to an artist, this was the one. I might also add that Steve also did most of the plotting after a while. Man, was I lucky to be working with guys like that.

People sometimes asked me if Dr. Strange was based on any magicians I had known. In truth, I must admit I personally knew very few Masters of the Mystic Arts, especially ones who are able to leave their bodies and travel to different dimensions in their ectoplasmic forms.

However, I still remember, as a kid of about eight years of age, being hooked on a radio serial called *Chandu, the Magician.* I don't really recall any details about it except that it featured a magician named Chandu who, I suppose, performed feats of magic. But, the one thing that does stick in my memory about that radio series is, the announcer would announce the title of the show in the most stentorian tones. After he said the name "Chandu" and added "the Magician" as loud and dramatically as he could, in his best Orson Welles tone of voice, a deafening cymbal would sound, like the gong that was struck at the opening of the old J. Arthur Rank movies. I can't tell you how that impressed me as a kid. I can still hear in my memory—"And now . . . Channnnnduuu, the MAGICIAN!" And then—"BONNNNNG!" That might be partly responsible for making such a cornball of me.

Writing *Dr. Strange* was a hoot because it gave me the opportunity to make up weird expressions for him to say. Let's suppose he wanted to cast a mystic spell. Now what would you imagine a real magician would say when casting a spell? "I'm gonna cast a spell?" Nope, that hasn't any flavor. "Abracadabra?" Uh-uh, it's too old and hackneyed. No, I liked to make up my own nutty-sounding expressions, such as "By the Hoary Hosts of Hoggoth, let the darkness shroud the light!" or, "By the Mystic Moons of Munnipor, may your weapons turn to sand!"

The funny part is, during many of my college lectures, there was always someone sure to ask "Stan, my frat brothers and I have been wondering, is it true that you based Dr. Strange's incantations on the writing of the ancient Druids?" Or, "I've been researching Dr. Strange's incantations and I feel you were obviously heavily influenced by translations from the Rosetta Stone and the Dead Sea Scrolls."

I hated having to admit that I just dreamed the stuff up simply because I liked to use phrases that sounded dramatic to me. Now that I think of it, I've probably disillusioned countless fans on the lecture circuit over the years. It might have been kinder to say I was kidnapped by a flying saucer and taught those incantations before being released. In fact, we can't be sure it didn't happen that way, can we?

Before 1963 had ended, we decided it was time for us to magnanimously bestow another new team of superheroes upon the eagerly waiting world. Once again I had to figure out a "scientific" way for a new group of characters to attain their superpowers. But this time I decided to take the cowardly way out.

It dawned on me that mutations often appear in nature, for no apparent reason. Okay, then, why couldn't I create a group of teenagers who had simply mutated and therefore gained some varied and extraordinary powers? No further explanation was needed, and I could introduce as many as we wanted because nature never set any limit on such things.

The title would be simplicity itself. I'd call our new group "The Mutants."

But simplicity is never as simple as it seems. Martin liked the concept but hated the title. He said our readers wouldn't know what a mutant was. Once again, a shining example of his high regard for the youthful reading public. I wasn't prepared to hassle with him over a title selection, so I tried to dream up another name, and then it hit me. They were heroes with *extra* powers. I had even named their adult mentor Professor *X*avier. So why not call them *The X-Men?*

This time Martin okayed the title although I never really understood his logic. If our readers wouldn't know what a mutant was, how would they know what an X-Man is? But I'm content to leave that capricious conundrum for future semanticists to ponder.

At the beginning of their series, the X-Men were youngsters who possessed various superpowers that did not burst forth until they became teenagers. This had deep and instant appeal to the average comicbook reader because many of them were teens, too. The fact that the

X-Men were also isolated from normal adult society played into the market as well, since most teens go through a period of emotional isolation as they mature.

The original group of X-Men consisted of Professor Xavier (the telepathic leader), the Angel (who flew with huge wings), Ice Man (who could freeze enemies), Marvel Girl (who was telekinetic), Cyclops (who could beam deadly rays out of his eyes), and Beast (who was intelligent, but had the power of a gorilla). Later, after Stan had stopped scripting the series, other innovative writers would add countless additional mutants such as Wolverine, Storm, Cable, Phoenix, and many more.

The Uncanny X-Men #1 opened with a memorable scene, magnificently delineated by artist Jack Kirby, which introduced the Danger Room, where the young mutants trained, enabling us to immediately display each X-Man's talent and give the new group of heroes a dramatic launch.

Jack and I didn't realize that the series would become as big as it did. After a few issues Jack, who had other strips to do, asked if I could get another penciller for the *X-Men*. Not wanting to overload our top artist, I said, "No problem. You stay with the other books you're doing." So, I gave the *X-Men* to different artists who were good, but they weren't Jack Kirby. Soon after, I also became too busy to stay with the book so I stopped writing it. Sales gradually began to slump.

Not long afterward, new artists and writers took over the strip. At one point, the talented Chris Claremont started writing it, Len Wein created Wolverine, and gifted artists like John Byrne did the illustrations. It got a new surge of popularity and, today, *The X-Men* is the best-selling group of comicbooks in the world.

Maybe Martin was right. *The X-Men* might have been a better title than I knew.

There must have been something in the air in 1963, because

in that same year we also gifted the reading public with *The Avengers.* It was another team of superheroes, but not new ones. Probably out of laziness, instead of dreaming up a whole kaboodle of new characters, I simply took our already established and popular Hulk, Thor, Iron Man, Ant Man, and the Wasp and had them form a team called the Avengers. In that first issue they battled Loki, the God of Evil—with a brief guest appearance by the Fantastic Four. The readers sure got their money's worth for 12¢, which was the cover price at that time.

Since Jolly Jack Kirby was familiar with all the main characters, it was natural for me to have him draw the series. As expected, *The Avengers* was an instant hit. Or, I could also say *The Avengers were* an instant hit. One version is grammatically correct; the other might sound better. Okay, now that I got that off my chest . . .

One great thing about *The Avengers* team is the fact that we could always change the line-up of heroes. We were able to send Iron Man on vacation and have Captain America come in to replace him. Then we had them kick out the Hulk because he became too unmanageable. Since kicking a Hulk out isn't easy to do, it became the basis for an action-packed story. Over the years, we've probably had every one of our heroes, and villains too, appearing in *The Avengers* from time to time. As you might imagine, my biggest problem was finding things for them to avenge, month after month.

The other major character that I cooked up during the same period is the blind superhero, Daredevil. I loved the idea of a blind man being able to accomplish things no sighted man could.

Luck was with me because my good friend Bill Everett, creator of the famous Sub-Mariner, was available to illustrate the first issue in his own inimitable style.

For Daredevil's origin, I'm embarrassed to say I fell back on the old device of radioactivity. As a teenager, some radioactive waste had spilled into Matt Murdock's eyes while he was saving someone's life. Although he lost his sight, the radioactivity caused his other senses to become greatly enhanced. For example, his sense of touch became so keen that he could "read" by moving his fingers over a printed page, actually feeling the imprint of the ink as if it were Braille. He could tell if people were lying to him by hearing their pulse speed up. His senses of taste and smell were likewise tremendously enhanced so that, although blind, there was virtually nothing he couldn't do. And, since I've read that it's something in our inner ear that enables us to balance ourselves, he's also the world's greatest gymnast. When I create a hero I don't kid around.

One thing worried me. I wondered if blind people would resent a character like Daredevil. After all, I was almost making it seem as if blindness could be an asset. I decided that at the very first indication that any blind person was offended, I'd drop the book. But the reaction was exactly the opposite of what I had feared.

Shortly after the first issue of *Daredevil, The Man Without Fear,* as I subtitled him, hit the stands, I started getting letters and calls from various charities and organizations that aided the blind. They were all positive, all commending us for depicting a handicapped man in such a positive light. I heard from many blind people who said they enjoyed having *Daredevil* read to them over and over again, and he was far and away their favorite hero and role model.

Happily, Matt Murdock and his costumed alter ego have remained one of our most popular heroes among sighted readers, too. It was a case of taking a really big gamble with a really unique character and having it pay off.

One story that Stan tells about his characters' names is worthy of inclusion here. He admits that he has always had a terrible memory. If he were an academician, he'd be the original absent-minded profes-

sor. *Therefore, since he created so many different characters over the years, and since he was aware how bad his memory was, he invented a system to help him remember the dozens and dozens of character names.*

The system was simplicity itself. Wherever possible, Stan would simply use the same letter for the first and last name. Thus we had Reed Richards, Bruce Banner, Matt Murdock, Peter Parker, Stephen Strange, etc. So, when Stan had to recall the name of a character, if he could remember just one of the names, he knew the other name began with the same letter and that would make it easier to bring it to memory.

Come to think of it, even in the case of his wife and daughter, he only has to remember the one name, Joan.

The early sixties was an era I'll never forget, a time of cascading creativity and escalating excitement. It was as though we could do nothing wrong. The ideas were tumbling out like confetti and the entire bullpen staff was caught up in all the excitement.

I felt as though everything was going perfectly. There was no reason to worry or be concerned about the company. Our characters were increasing in popularity every day. Our sales figures were growing by leaps and bounds. Our future was assured. We just had to keep doing what we were doing and the future would take care of itself.

Boy, was I ever wrong!

Transition, Trouble, and Travel

By 1965, Marvel Comics and Stan had come out of the financial doldrums. Marvel was making money and had become wildly popular, even beyond the preteen set. Stan's own popularity was becoming legend and his constant comments about the bullpen staff in his columns and interviews served to make the artists and writers well-known and popular with the fans as well.

Yet, despite Marvel's unprecedented success, tensions were building beneath the surface.

The workload that Stan was carrying grew increasingly heavy, and the pressure resulted in a problem of time management. Stan was not only Marvel's editor-in-chief and art director, he was still writing the dialogue and captions for a majority of the stories. But unfortunately, time management wasn't the only problem Stan faced in those hectic times. There was another management problem named Steve Ditko.

Little by little I noticed that Steve was beginning to give off hostile vibes. At first I thought it was my imagination, but after a while I realized that something was bugging him. Steve wasn't the most communicative guy in the world, and to this day I'm not quite sure what the problem was. It just seemed to me that he had a growing resentment toward me and the work I did, particularly in connection with *Spider-Man*. This certainly wasn't a healthy situation, as together we were responsible for producing the most important title that Marvel was turning out. As far as I can guess, part of the problem was that I was the editor at Marvel as well as the writer. When reporters wanted to do a story about Marvel and *Spider-Man*, I was the one they inevitably came to interview. I often suggested that they talk to Steve as well, but it turned out that he didn't really want to be interviewed; he was a very private person. So, since it was my job to keep Marvel and all our strips in the public's eye as much as possible, I was the one the press became familiar with, and it was my name that became irrevocably linked with *Spider-Man*.

Although, when interviewed, I always mentioned Steve's importance in regard to *Spider-Man*, the stories that appeared in magazines and newspapers often made it seem as if *Spider-Man* was a one-man show and I was that man.

When Roy Thomas joined Marvel as an editor/writer, he noticed the growing tension. As he said later, "Everybody was walking on eggs around Steve Ditko by the time I arrived, because he and Stan had not been speaking for months. They continued working together on Spider-Man, *but the material and messages on the strip were passed back and forth through the mail and other people."*

Finally, in 1966, Steve left Marvel.

Now, a third of a century later, as I think back on that time, I'm still sorry about the fact that Steve may have felt slighted. I never wanted it that way. Even today, whenever I talk about the origin of *Spider-Man*, I always say I started it with Steve Ditko. I tell everyone that after I came up with the basic concept and the cast of characters, I selected Steve, out of all the artists I could have chosen, because he not only had the perfect illustrative style for designing the characters and creating the look of the strip but his plotting input was also extraordinarily valuable.

In fact, some time ago, suspecting that Steve was still bothered by not getting what he feels is his proper share of the credit for *Spider-Man*, I sent him a letter in which I acknowledged that he was the cocreator of *Spider-Man* and told him he could feel free to show that letter to anyone he chose, hoping that would make him feel better.

As I've mentioned before, I really think I'm being very generous in giving him "cocreator" credit, because I'm the guy who dreamed up the title, the concept, and the characters.

But, to be fair to Steve, here's his point of view. He feels that all I had was an idea. Until it was put down on illustration board and given form and shape, it was nothing more than an idea. An idea in a vacuum is just an idea until the artist brings it to life, sayeth Mr. Ditko.

Personally, I still think the idea is the thing, because an idea can be given to any artist to be brought to life. However, even though I feel he has confused the "creation" of a strip with its "execution," I'm more than willing to say that Steve cocreated the web-swinger with me, and I hope the matter will now be peacefully laid to rest.

Not that Ditko and Stan were the only ones who had disagreements. Stan had a similar problem with another of his key artists, Jack Kirby, who also began to resent the spotlight that was shining on Stan. This resentment grew over the years, especially after Jack left Marvel for good at the end of 1978.

As Kirby grew older, and as his art attracted critical acclaim in its own right, he began to insist to fan magazines that Stan's creative and editorial role at Marvel was minimal. Rather, Kirby maintained that he had really been running the show at Marvel all along, drawing the strips without input or editorial oversight from Stan. Jack even went as far as to say that Stan would never dare edit any of his artwork or ask him to redraw anything.

Luckily, John Romita, who was working in our office during those days, has a good memory. When he heard what Kirby had charged, and he heard me say, "Wow, I can't believe Jack would say that I never edited any of his artwork. If only I could remember some specific instances . . ."

John said to me, "Stan, don't you recall? Whenever an inker applied for work, we'd give him some rejected penciled pages to ink as a test. Luckily, there were always plenty of those pages laying around the office that we'd use for that purpose. Where do you think those pages came from? Lots of them were Kirby's; pages that you had rejected and made him do over again because you felt they weren't quite right. I clearly remember that you used to edit his stuff all the time."

Well, that certainly made me feel better. Not that I harbored much resentment against Jack for some of the things he was saying. I was aware that there were people who, for whatever reason, continually told him that Marvel was taking advantage of him, not appreciating him enough, not giving him enough credit for what he did. Unfortunately, whenever anyone became unhappy with Marvel, I was the logical guy to take it out on.

I've been asked if it would have been possible to salvage my relationship with either Jack Kirby or Steve Ditko. I think it would have been if either of them were less laconic. There was never a time when Jack Kirby just sat down and told me what, if anything, was bothering him. The same held true for Steve Ditko. It's hard to correct a misunderstanding if you don't know what it is that's misunderstood.

I've also heard that some people tried to inflame Jack by telling him that I earned more money than he. It's true. I did. But the situation wasn't that cut-and-dried.

Jack was paid as a freelancer for his artwork. I too was paid on a freelance basis, for my scripts. We were both paid "by the page."

Jack's penciling rate per page was far higher than my script rate, but I could write faster than he could draw so it pretty much evened out. But the reason I earned more was—I was also the editor and art director, for which I received an additional salary.

But here's the ironic part. Many times in the past I had asked Jack to take an executive staff job at Marvel. I felt if he were willing, I'd give him my art director duties; he could supervise the artwork and I'd concentrate on the editing and handle the scripts. We would be full partners with his salary equaling mine.

However, Jack never accepted the offer. He told me he'd prefer to freelance. I was disappointed because I felt that the two of us, working as a team, would have been dynamite. But that's what irritates me about people telling Jack how unfair it was that I made more money than he. He could have had exactly the same financial arrangement as I did, but he never accepted it.

Of course, it might not have worked out as well as I would have hoped. I have very definite feelings and taste about artwork, and I'm sure Jack had, too. Both of us were very strong willed. If we disagreed about the way a strip should be drawn or who should draw it, who knows what problems might have arisen?

Perhaps it's better that I handled the art and editorial chores alone. I may not always have been right, but I never argued with my own decisions.

Such disputes aside, progress at Marvel continued unabated. In 1966, Marvel made the transition from comicbooks to animated cartoons when several characters debuted on Saturday morning TV in The Marvel Super Heroes *show. The animation wasn't exactly Disney quality, but in some crazy way, the cartoons captured the spirit of Marvel.*

Meanwhile, things were beginning to change in Stan and Joan's personal lives as well. While they loved their home and their friends in Hewlett Harbor, their daughter wanted to experience the excite-

ment of the big city and Stan was tiring of the long commute into town. The idea of walking to work again grew more appealing, and thus, the Lees returned to Manhattan.

An unexpected phone call from my brother Larry told us, in a voice trembling with sorrow, that my father, who never remarried and had been living in Manhattan all these years, had died unexpectedly. We felt a sudden emptiness as we realized we could look forward to no more visits from him.

That was when I decided that twenty years is a long time to be at any one place. That's how long Joanie and I had lived in Hewlett Harbor. Our daughter, Joanie C., had grown up there and was now eighteen and wanted to move to Manhattan. After a lot of discussion, we decided that it made sense for us, too. So we sold our house and all three headed for the Big Apple.

When we moved to Manhattan, where we would stay till 1980, we bought a condo in the East 60s—in fact, we moved from one to another about three times during that period, each time getting a somewhat better view and a somewhat bigger terrace. However, each one of our pads was in that same East 60s area because Joanie, my little black-belt, world-class shopper, didn't want to live anywhere that wasn't within walking distance of the Bloomingdale's department store at Sixtieth Street and Third Avenue.

I remember the last condo we had, on Sixty-third Street. It was on the fourteenth floor with an enormous terrace. Actually, it was more than just a terrace; it was one of the building's setbacks. Joanie bought green, wall-to-wall outdoor carpeting for the floor and placed potted trees all along the outer walls. It was as close as we could get to a real country feeling. Even today, many years later, whenever I have a few spare minutes on a visit to New York, I make it a point to walk along Third Avenue to Sixty-third Street and look up at what used to be our old terrace, because I still get a kick out of seeing that all those trees are still there.

Some people asked me if, at that period, we felt we had "ar-

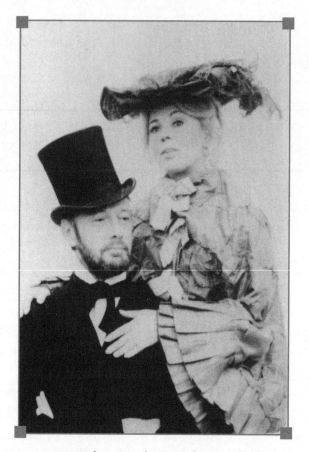

**You can imagine how tough it was for the photographer
to get us to pose during a costume party.**

rived," but I didn't really know what that meant. We never thought about things that way, about arriving. We just took one day at a time, my wife and daughter keeping busy with the myriad things they did and me wrapped up in my work.

As far as the word "arrived" is concerned, I wasn't aware of anything to arrive at in comicbooks. I just kept writing my stories, dealing with the creative staff, doing interviews, working on the

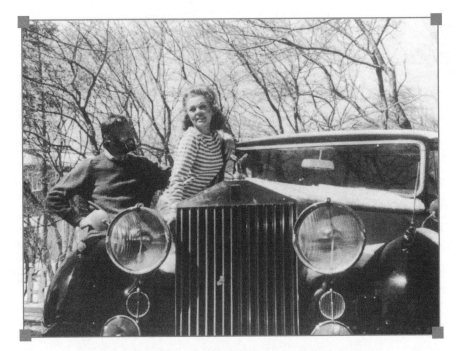

We always had a love affair with beautiful, classic cars.
A pity that this one was borrowed.

fan mail, and hoping the books would sell. At the end of the day I went home, spent time with Joanie, had dinner, watched some television, and often did some more writing after my wife fell asleep.

In fact, when this whole biography thing was proposed to me, I was afraid it wouldn't have enough sex and violence to interest anyone. I've never done drugs, haven't had affairs with most of the stars in Hollywood—or any of them, for that matter—and wouldn't tell if I did. Nor have I been in and out of rehabs. The Lee family's doings aren't exactly the stuff of which the *National Enquirer* articles are made. But if you're game to stay with it, so am I. Let's see where all this is heading . . .

The Sultan of Strips

With Marvel's tremendous sales, the company was zooming up and getting more and more attention in financial circles, as could be expected. Marvel's expansion into television increased its popularity with the fans so that, by 1968, they were moving 50 million copies of their comicbooks every year, while Stan had a great time narrating many of the cartoons.

Following the financial philosophy of buying low and selling high, Martin Goodman decided it was the right time to sell his company.

In the autumn of 1968 the big news in the life of Stan and his colleagues was the sale of Marvel to the Perfect Film and Chemical Corporation. Goodman was to stay on as president and publisher of Magazine Management, the holding company's new publishing wing, but not Marvel. Stan didn't know how he'd be affected but hoped the change would be for the better, because Marvel would now be part of a financially strong conglomerate.

Goodman's timing was perfect because, the next year, the whole industry took a dip as all the comic publishers raised prices from twelve cents to fifteen cents a copy. Stan didn't realize that this development would mark the beginning of a long, hard journey that would ultimately see a company and people he loved torn and trampled.

Chapter 15

Stan was curious to see what was going to happen next. At first, he looked at the new events with his usual optimism, feeling that the company must be doing well for somebody to pay a lot of money for it. Wasn't that a sign of success in America? He learned later that the short answer can be "no."

Martin told me that Perfect Film was offering him between $12 and $15 million in cash for Marvel because he wanted all cash; he wasn't interested in stocks. Remember, that was back in 1968, when $15 million was probably better than $100 million today.

But here's the kicker. Perfect told Martin they wouldn't buy the company unless I signed a contract to stay on. They regarded me as a key employee and didn't want the deal unless they knew I came with it. I had never been under contract before and thought the notion was pretty damn flattering. I couldn't wait to tell Joanie.

One of my closest friends, who also happened to be a brilliant businessman, was Marshall Finck, chairman of the board of a major company. He told me I was in a great position since my being under contract was "of the essence" for the sale being made. Marshall said I could ask Martin for almost anything and he would have to give it to me.

Well, Stan "Big Brain" Lee shrugged Marshall off by saying, "Are you kidding? Martin may have his faults, but he's a friend. I've worked for him for twenty years. Do you think I'd insult him by saying, 'What are you going to give me?' I know he'll be fair. I'm not some money-grubbing ingrate who's gonna take advantage of the situation."

Marshall just shook his head sadly, sighed, and walked away.

So I signed the contract. It was for a three-year term and provided for a raise in salary. Period. Yep, that was me—Stan Lee, sharp negotiator, shrewd judge of character, and trusting soul.

I remember the next night when Joanie and I had dinner at the Goodmans' house. We lived nearby and Joanie was very friendly with Martin's wife, my cousin Jean. We were walking down the stairs to their den and Martin put his arm around my shoulders and said, "Stan, I'll see to it that you and Joanie will never have to want for anything as long as you live." That sounded good.

A short time later, he put his arm around my shoulders again and said, "Stan, I'm going to make you a gift of some valuable warrants," which he said were somewhat like stock options. I figured, At last. This is my pot of gold. He's keeping his promise. And how nice, without my having to ask.

As time went by, the warrants proved to be absolutely worthless. But what was even worse—although he said he would, he never actually gave them to me. I couldn't quite get over that. Not only did they turn out to have no value, but I never got them anyhow. Nor did he ever, in any way, make good on that promise that Joanie and I would never want for anything as long as we live. No bonus. No bonds. No warrants, either worthless or otherwise. Zilch.

I guess there's a lesson to be learned there somewhere. But hey, life goes on.

One of my lifelong regrets is that I've always been too casual about money. It's been made abundantly clear to me, by friends such as Marshall and others, that I should have realized I was creating a whole kaboodle of characters that became valuable franchises, but I was creating them for others.

I can still hear Marshall saying, "Why didn't you ever quit and form your own company? It wouldn't have been hard for you to get backing."

But such an idea would have been alien to me. I guess that somewhere in my subconscious there has always been the image of my father, out of work, worried every month about where the rent money would come from, desperately wishing he could find a job.

To me, just having a good, steady job, feeling that I was

wanted, needed by some company, was the ultimate mark of success, of security.

When it comes to competition, I'm one guy the companies listed in the *Forbes* 500 will never have to worry about.

Soon, Perfect Film's stockholders and board of directors forced out the company's chief executive, Martin Ackerman, and installed Sheldon Feinberg in his place. Feinberg changed the name of the company from Perfect Film to Cadence Industries, which he subsequently controlled for several years. Martin Goodman stayed on as president of Magazine Management, but Sheldon Feinberg was the man in charge. Unfortunately, Feinberg was no different from Ackerman or Martin Goodman before him in the sense of having a vision for the company. Although Stan had built Marvel up as the best-selling comicbook company, the new owners never seemed to know how to fully capitalize on Marvel's success.

Nevertheless, the Cadence management did recognize Stan's amazing creativity, his rapport with his audience, and his genius for promotion, so they made him an offer that he couldn't refuse.

After that eye-opening incident with my big-hearted boss, I felt it was now really time to quit. I didn't know where I'd go or what I'd do, but it would have been impossible to just carry on as though I hadn't been so royally screwed.

But life has a way of always tossing zingers at you when you least expect them.

Unexpectedly, Marvel's new owners did something for me that caught me completely by surprise. They offered me the job of publisher!

It was a proposition that I felt would open a whole new world for me, allow me to do some things for Marvel that I'd always wanted to do. Deep down, I had never really wanted to leave Marvel. I'd been there for three decades. I always thought of it as home, as the place I'd work at as long as I was able to work.

But once again Martin proved what a friend and grateful guy he was. He tried every way he could to prevent my becoming publisher because he had been hoping to give that job to his son, Chip.

Chip was actually a good guy. He was Martin's youngest son, who had worked at the place for a few years in the so-called "slick magazine" department and had no actual experience with comics. He was bright and would probably have done as good a job as any other inexperienced man in that position.

Still, despite all Martin could do, Cadence went ahead with their offer and named me publisher of Marvel Comics.

What I'm about to tell now is still hard, after all these years, for me to accept, but I swear it's true. When my promotion was announced, Martin actually had the gall to accuse me of disloyalty, of betraying him after all he had done for me. By then, I was beginning to realize that the fantasy tales I wrote might be more credible than some of the things that seemed to happen in my real life.

Needless to say, by this time I didn't care what Martin said or thought. I was finally free to do what I had always felt could and should be done with Marvel, and that was all that mattered.

The one thing I always thought our company lacked was the right type of promotion. We had heroes whom our readers loved; we had enthusiasts who couldn't wait for the next issues of their favorite titles; we had as solid a corps of fans as any company could hope for; but we never had a meaningful program in place for promoting or publicizing our product. Except for our fans, most of the outside world seemed blissfully unaware of us.

I knew the so-called Marvel style was now thoroughly ingrained among our staff. I knew our artists, writers, and editors were the best in the business. I knew that the groundwork had been laid; it shouldn't be necessary for me to personally do as much writing or editing any longer. I had the utmost faith in the incredibly talented staff we had been lucky enough to acquire throughout the years. Most of all, I knew what I now had to do.

So, as publisher, I turned over most of the creative work to others, chief among them an enormously talented young writer/editor named Roy Thomas whom I appointed as editor-in-chief. Being able to hand over the reins to someone as trustworthy and competent as Roy was a great break for me. It freed me up to begin devoting myself to promoting Marvel as I had always felt it should be promoted. I wanted to bring our company to the next plateau, to make it the next Disney.

For the first time, Stan stopped writing most of the books and spent years just promoting Marvel. For the next decade and a half, he traveled all over the country, fifty-two weeks a year, averaging a minimum of one lecture a week, speaking to full houses at colleges and universities throughout the United States, Canada, and Europe. By Stan's estimation, he has probably lectured at least once at every university and college in the United States alone.

Stan's reception on so many campuses led to growing interest in the mainstream media about Marvel's characters. In their main caption atop a double spread, for instance, Esquire *magazine quoted college students as saying, "We think of Stan Lee as today's Homer." Besides helping to separate Marvel from the competition, the end result was, due in a large part to Stan's unceasing efforts, that comicbooks as a group were beginning to become respectable, were beginning to be considered a legitimate part of American culture.*

Marvel artist John Romita Sr. once said, "I used to hide the fact that I was in comics. We used to say we were in commercial illustration rather than admit to being comicbook artists. It wasn't until the 1960s that I started telling people how proud I was of my comics industry." And to be sure, as Stan traveled through the groves of academe, he began to discover that the more intelligent students were actually among his biggest fans. The students never failed to impress him with their deep knowledge of Marvel's characters and their ability to draw points of connection between Stan's works and the tradition of Western art, mythology, and literature.

Since I was the only person devoting so much time and energy to promoting a comicbook company, I became somewhat well-known by the press. Feature writers, always looking for offbeat stories, were constantly calling me to talk about the effect of comics on young people, about the fact that comicstrips—along with jazz—were one of the true American art forms, about what it's like to produce comics, and countless other subjects of that type. After a while, many writers started referring to me as "Mr. Marvel." I kinda liked that.

My first invitation to speak on a campus came from Bard College in New York. I was so impressed at actually being invited to speak at a college that I attempted to dress as carefully as possible, putting on my best suit and most elegant tie. When I arrived at Bard, I found that most of the students were dressed like hippies; beards, torn undershirts, army fatigues—well, it was the sixties, you know the scene. I probably stood out as the year's biggest nerd. Luckily, however, the occasion went well and after my speech I was enthusiastically asked to stay for dinner with a whole gaggle of students and profs.

My next invitation was to Princeton. This time I wasn't about to be Stan the Square. So, I donned my oldest pair of jeans, a faded T-shirt, and a pair of worn sneakers. Well, wouldn't you know it, I was invited to a formal dinner at the dean's residence where everyone was dressed like Cary Grant! But those guys were great. They pretended not to notice that their guest speaker was Stan the Slob. In fact, some of the students later made me an honorary member of the Princeton Cliosophic and Debating Society. I may not have known what that meant but you can bet I had my certificate framed and gave it a place of honor on my office wall.

To me, the lecture tour was fun, exciting, eye-opening, and educational. One of the best parts was visiting so many foreign countries. I've spoken in Japan, Italy, Canada, Germany, Poland, Spain, Denmark, France, Portugal, and even China.

One of the most impressive events was in Mexico City, where they provided me with six, count 'em, six bodyguards. I asked if that was because Marvel had lots of enemies there. But they said it was to protect me from the crowd. I couldn't believe it until we reached the place where I was to lecture. It looked like a palace. There was a huge lawn in front, protected by big gates. You had to go through the gates and up the lawn to the impressive entrance.

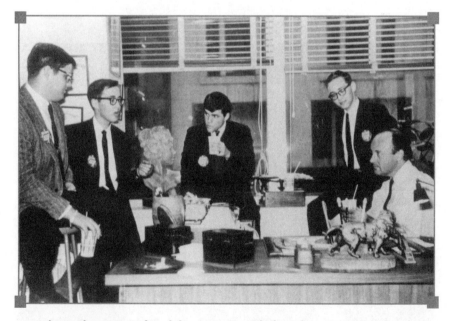

In the mid-sixties, a fan delegation accorded me honorary membership
in the Princeton University Cliosophic and Debating Society.
They gained immediate admittance because they each wore a
Merry Marvel Marching Society button!

I arrived there in an entourage of cars. After stopping, I got out accompanied by my six bodyguards. They walked ahead of me, opened the gates, and there on both sides of an enormous lawn were fifteen thousand cheering adults and kids!

The guards plowed a path through them like the parting of the Red Sea. As I was walking through with three big guys on each side of me, people kept yelling, "*Olé! Olé!* Stan Lee! Stan Lee! Marvel! Marvel! Sign this! Sign this! Wait! *Por favor*—a picture! Let me take your picture, shake your hand!" It was unbelievable. I'll never forget it. One of the guards said, "Stan, I swear, you could run for president and you'd be elected right here and now."

Sorry to say I wasn't elected, but don't anyone ever try to tell me comicbooks haven't great influence!

After being on the lecture circuit for more than ten years, I re-

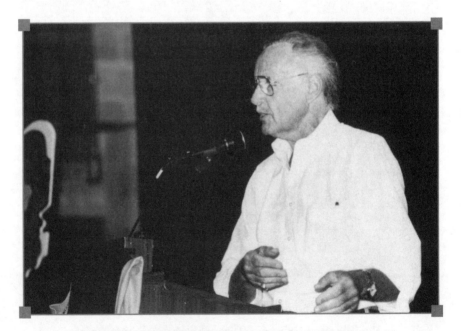

Making a speech is almost better than being an actor—
you don't haveta worry about the critics' reviews.

alized I had to slow down. It was taking too much out of me. Even though it had reached the point where schools and organizations were paying me to speak and I had to be represented by a lecture bureau, even though I eventually kept raising my speaking fee, hoping it would cut down on the amount of lectures I had to give, the invitations kept pouring in.

Finally, I just gave it up. No more lectures. After more than a decade, I didn't want to be guilty of overkill. By then, if there was anyone in the civilized world who didn't know about Marvel Comics, it just wasn't my fault!

Friends Are Forever

In 1970, Martin Goodman left the company.

The company's new corporate owner, Cadence Industries, replaced him with a revolving succession of executives. In 1975, Jim Galton, who had previously headed a paperback publishing line, joined the team, remaining as president until 1990. Stan and Galton got along beautifully: Galton took care of the business end, leaving Stan free to create. Stan had often said that Jim was one of Marvel's most competent executives and a good friend, as well.

While living in Manhattan, Stan and Joanie bought a small house in the Hamptons where they would go on weekends. Four of their closest friends, Murray and Dorothy Platt, and Marshall and Edie Finck, also had homes there. It was a wonderful time for the Lees, with beach parties, hiking, riding their mopeds, and just generally hanging out and enjoying each other's company. The only problem was the heavy traffic from New York to the Hamptons every weekend on the Long Island Expressway, which New Yorkers referred to as the world's longest parking lot. Stan used to say that he and his friends spent more time planning when to leave in order to beat the traffic than they did on anything else. But then, he would say with a grin, at least it gave us something to talk about.

Chapter 16

Two of our closest friends were Lee and Marge Ross. Lee was a successful home builder on Long Island and Marge was the daughter of the famous judge, Samuel Leibowitz, who, as an attorney, had defended the Scottsboro boys and taken on many other high-profile cases. A best-selling book, *Courtroom*, had been written about him by Quentin Reynolds and it had later been made into a movie. Both Marge and Lee have since divorced and remarried, but they still remain good friends with us and each other. Marge moved to Beverly Hills a few years before Joanie and I came to California, and we still see a lot of each other.

I'd need another book to tell about our many close friends, all of whom are so very important to us. There are Ken and Kaye Bald, two of the best-looking and most decent human beings on the planet. I remember first meeting Ken, in my early days at Marvel. He was a war hero who had just been mustered out of the marines, where he had served as an officer in the Pacific. He was the handsomest male I had ever seen and, judging by his artwork, he was also one of the most talented. On top of all that, his wife, Kaye, was a glamorous actress who had starred in motion pictures. Is it any wonder I hated him on sight? Well, that was then. For about half a century we've been the closest friends and my only regret is that the Balds now live in New Jersey to be near their many children and grandchildren, and we don't see them as often as we'd want to. Oh, don't let me forget to mention that Ken was the first to do Timely's *Millie the Model*. Alas, instead of staying in comics he left to become a top advertising illustrator, which was definitely our loss.

I had a similar experience with another dear friend, Jim Mooney. Jim, too, came to the office one day to offer to draw for us. Like Ken, his artwork was terrific. Also like Ken, he was a handsome, sharp-tongued, devil-may-care Irishman who was married to a glamorous female, an ex-Broadway showgirl. Jim took great pains to brag that he could write, draw, color, and even letter our strips if need be. With my hackles rising, I growled, "Can you work the printing presses, too?" He snapped back, "Yeah, if I had to!" Again, just like with Ken, after an initial meeting where we almost came to blows we became the very best of friends. Jim also did many terrific strips for us, but he had many other interests such as sculpting, painting, and antiquing. He used to drag Joanie and me to antique shows and flea markets ad nauseam. Joanie loved it and I hated every minute of it, but she was my best wife and he was one of my best friends, so what the hell. Unfortunately, Jim now lives in Florida, just to spite me, I think.

My demon accountant, Irwin Shapiro, also lives three thousand miles away from me in Larchmont, New York. Though he knows as little about comics as I do about accounting, he and his lovely Swedish wife, Ingala, have been the closest of friends with Joanie and me for more years than I can remember.

I'll never forget when they came out to L.A. recently and Irr, as I call him, wanted to go to the Universal Studios theme park. When we got there, I said to the ticket seller, for the first time in my life, "Two senior citizen tickets, please." Boy, Irr and I were never so angry in our lives. The girl sold us the tickets without even asking for IDs! She believed that we were over fifty. I don't know how Universal stays in business with help like that.

Then there was the Alexanders, Mel and Sandy. Mel was my insurance agent and pal, not necessarily in that order. He was also a top golfer at the Seawane Club in Hewlett Harbor, to which we belonged, which didn't hurt his insurance business one bit. His wife, Sandy, was a tall, blond, strikingly beautiful model who has been one of Joanie's closest friends for decades. When Mel and Sandy ultimately divorced, she married Gene Pope, who was the owner of the *National Enquirer* at the time. I'll never forget an incident that occurred . . .

Joanie and I often went to Manhattan's famous Stork Club for dinner. One night, as we were leaving, we passed Sandy and Gene who were there at a table with Frank Costello, reputedly one of the nation's most powerful gang leaders. When Gene introduced us, I froze, wondering what to say. Somehow, "I've heard a lot about you" didn't seem like the right thing. I couldn't get the words, "A pleasure to meet you," out, either. After sweating it for a few seconds, I finally settled for "How d'ya do?" which was as noncommittal as I could get, and then Joanie and I made it to the exit as fast as possible. Never did find out what he was doing there.

Another colorful guy is my lawyer friend, Peter Bierstedt, who, luckily, lives in L.A. with his lovely wife, Lieschen. None of my friends seem to be truly normal and Peter is no exception. He takes about four or five vacations a year, but instead of going where sane tourists go, he and Lieschen head for spots like the headhunters section of Borneo, the forbidden areas of Tibet, the wilds of Siberia, or wherever there are man-eating tigers or waters filled with killer sharks. However, Peter does have one redeeming virtue; he finally stopped asking us to go with him.

Then there was Batman creator Bob Kane. Joanie and I regularly had dinner with the talented, loquacious Bob and his charming actress wife Elizabeth, often together with that most prolific and amusing writer/director Larry Cohen and his equally charming Cynthia. But it was always a contest. You see, the Kanes seemed to be pathologically incapable of arriving at a restaurant on time. So we would try to be a few minutes late ourselves in order to match their arrival. But no matter how late we were, they managed to arrive even later. It reached the point where the only way to beat them was not to show up at all. They finally won our last contest by not appearing till we'd finished dinner and telling us they'd gone to the wrong restaurant!

Another big talent who lives right nearby but I never see as often as I'd like to is the brilliant, barb-witted, best-selling and best-writing author I know, the eternal burr in the side of phoniness and pomposity, Harlan Ellison. I've rarely had more fun than the few times the two of us held forth at various conventions, debating and just kidding around on stage. Ahh, those good ol' days.

Speaking of good old days, there are a few more wonderful guys who are no longer with us, but I've got to mention them. I met Sandy Schwarz when he worked as an ad salesman for Martin Goodman, before he formed his own successful ad company. He was the smartest, most well-informed, most interesting guy imaginable, also the most forgiving. I'll never forget the day he bought a new car. He brought it to Joanie and me to show it off. He was indescribably proud of it. Joanie asked if she could drive it around the block. He said "Sure." She brought it back a couple of minutes later with a dented fender! And he still remained one of our best friends!

Bob Fenton's the other great guy whom Joanie and I miss tremendously. A young, ex-West Pointer, he had been our neighbor in Hewlett Harbor. He was the funniest, most entertaining human we'd ever known. Life to him was a never-ending party. He was popularity personified; everybody liked him, but everyone was sure he'd never amount to anything because he took nothing seriously. Since life is totally unpredictable, he ended up owning a string of radio stations on the West Coast as well as a yacht and a private airplane. We could just imagine if he had been more serious—he'd probably have become king of the world!

One day I had bought a new sports jacket and wore it to a restaurant with Bob, his lovely wife, Jane, and, of course, Joanie. Bob kept noticing that I made a funny noise every time I moved my arms. After a while, everyone noticed it but no one could tell where it came from. It was finally Bob who realized it was coming from inside the jacket itself. The tailor had accidentally sewn the paper containing the blueprint, or whatever the hell it is that they use in designing clothes, inside of the lining!

My cousin Morty Feldman is another terrific guy. He lives

in Dallas, where he's been in the ladies' hat business for years. Since virtually none of the women I know wear hats anymore, I've always felt he might as well be making mustache wax or buggy whips, but the son of a gun somehow does pretty well, taking long vacation trips every year with his vivacious lady, Mikki, and continually writing me letters that I can't understand because he's got the world's worst handwriting. Luckily Mikki can use e-mail, so that's made our relationship more comprehensible lately.

Nor can I omit Murray and Dottie Platt. Murray owned an electronics company that he eventually sold to Continental Telephone for a bundle. It occurs to me that it's strange how many of our closest friends were business people. But the thing I'll always remember about the Platts is the day Joanie and I met them. We all felt it would be the start of a real friendship, and Murray enthusiastically told me that he could get us season tickets to the opera, and concerts, and—I stopped him then and there. "Murray," said I, "I hate the opera and wouldn't go to a concert if you paid me. If we're gonna be friends, never mention those awful words again." Y'know something? He never did. But the four of us spent tons of time together, especially out in the Hamptons.

There's no way to describe how much you can miss old friends.

There's also no way to describe how awful I'll feel when, after this book has gone to press, I'll remember all the other people who've been so very important to me and who I stupidly forgot to mention this time around. Well, there's only one solution. Sooner or later I'll have to hit you with a sequel!

But I fear I've digressed.

As time went by and Marvel continued to grow more and more popular, I was approached by other syndicates, asking if I'd write newspaper strip versions of some of our own top comicbook characters, especially Spider-Man.

I was reluctant to take any of them up on their offers. First of all, I didn't want to be in a position where they could tell me things like, "Green's a nice color, but I think I'd like you to change the Hulk's skin to purple."

But there was an even stronger reason. The "pacing" of a newspaper strip is totally different from that of a comicbook strip. In comicbooks, we generally have at least twenty pages, averaging five or six panels each, in which to tell our story. In the newspapers, you only have two or three panels the reader can see in one day. That doesn't even allow you to have a decent fight scene. Picture this: in panel three of Tuesday's strip, Captain America punches a spy. In panel one of Wednesday's strip, the spy falls down from the punch! Not very satisfying continuity, right?

So I turned down any and all offers because I couldn't figure out how to get the Marvel brand of action and excitement in two or three panels a day. But the whole matter continued to bug me. I knew it would be good for us to be represented in newspapers all around the world. So I kept working on the problem in my spare time, trying to figure out a way to tell our type of story in the newspaper strip format.

Finally, Denny Allen, president of the Register & Tribune Syndicate, which has since been absorbed by King Features, contacted me with a tempting offer. He said if I'd do a seven-days-a-week version of *Spider-Man* for his syndicate he'd give me a totally free hand to do it any way I wanted to. His timing was perfect because, by then, I thought I had figured out a way to make it work. So I agreed.

For those who can keep a secret, I'll confess that, since I realized there's no satisfactory way to do the sort of lengthy fight scenes in a daily newspaper strip that are done in comicbooks, I decided to treat the *Spider-Man* strip like a soap opera. I played down the action scenes and played up the human interest and personal relationships, without omitting the colorful villains, of course. Right or wrong, it seemed to work.

And so, in January of 1977, Spider-Man, *the syndicated strip, first appeared in newspapers around the country and later around the world. Stan selected John Romita, with whom he had discussed the strip idea for years, to be the initial artist. An enormous success, the strip appeared in more than two hundred papers within its first month and eventually leveled off at about five hundred papers a month worldwide, which was a tremendous achievement for a story strip since they usually don't do as well as humor strips in newspaper syndication.*

One last thing about the Spider-Man *strip. It became the most popular, most successful, and longest lived of any strip featuring a superhero. In fact, Stan still writes it today, with his artist brother, Larry Lieber, penciling the dailies.*

Indeed, the 1970s were to become an unusually busy decade in Stan's already hectic life, as he continued to explore new comicbook formats. In 1978, and despite some of their previous friction, Stan reunited with Jack Kirby on a project that Stan had been nurturing for several years, a novel-length version of The Silver Surfer, *who had long been one of Stan's favorite characters.*

Luckily, the rift between Stan and Jack was never as bad as the fan magazine columnists claimed, and Jack was eager to collaborate once more with Stan on a project that excited them both. Stan had gotten Simon & Schuster to agree to publish his and Jack's version of The Silver Surfer *in book form as a legitimate graphic novel, perhaps the first time a comicbook character had been presented in such an impressive format.*

Something else important for Marvel and for Stan occurred at the start of 1978. After a quick succession of nearly a half-dozen editors, a longtime fan named Jim Shooter signed on as editor-in-chief,

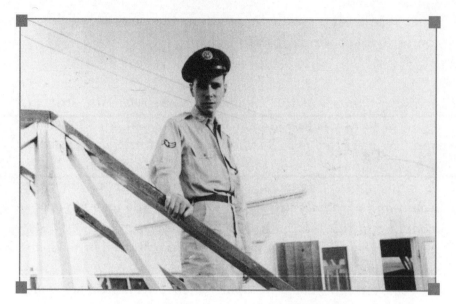

My brother, Larry, in service in Okinawa during the Korean War.
With each of us serving the U.S.A. in different wars,
Americans were able to sleep more securely.

where he would stay through the 1980s, giving Stan still more time to busy himself with a myriad of other projects.

Jim Shooter was an interesting and amazing guy in many ways. For openers, he had been laid up in a hospital when he was a kid and read comicbooks while he was getting well. This turned him on to the world of comics so much that he became a comicbook writer at age fourteen! That's younger than I was when I started. He was entranced by comicbooks, but especially by Marvel comics, beginning with *The Amazing Spider-Man* #2. So, he caught the comicbook bug, and by 1966, as a teenager, he had sold several Superman stories to DC Comics.

Jim and I had a good personal relationship. He was only eighteen when I hired him as a writer in 1969, but I was the last one who would ever be influenced by anyone's age, whether old or young. He wrote for us and then for other companies, but in 1978, when I saw there was a chance of getting him as editor-in-chief, I hired him on the spot. The important thing was for him to get along well with Jim Galton, and at that time he did.

Under Galton's business leadership, Stan's characters continued to make the move to television. An animated version of The Fantastic Four *appeared on NBC in 1978, with Stan collaborating on scripts with Roy Thomas, who had served briefly as Marvel's editor-in-chief before deciding that the writing life was his true calling.*

Galton's negotiations with movie and television studios began to pay off as a live-action version, The Amazing Spider-Man, *played by Nicholas Hammond, premiered on CBS about the same time, followed by* Dr. Strange *in 1978 and* Captain America *in 1979. While these programs proved short-lived, owing in part to the networks' sporadic scheduling, one of Marvel's new live-action shows—* The Incredible Hulk—*was a surprise critical hit and enduring fan favorite.*

The TV version of the *Hulk* owes much of its success to the talented guy who wrote it. Writer/director Ken Johnson was smart enough to take something that could have been somewhat corny—I mean, a green monster running around and shouting, "Hulk mad! Hulk smash!"—and turn it into an engrossing, dramatic show for an adult audience, without losing the younger fans.

Ken wisely decided that the Hulk wouldn't speak at all in the series, which immediately eliminated the "Hulkese" that worked okay for comics but would have been laughable on screen. He made another wise decision. If you remember, there were only about five or six minutes when you actually saw the Hulk in the whole sixty-minute show. The rest of the hour dealt with mature, dramatic situations, centered around the talented and charismatic Bill Bixby, as fine an actor as one could wish for, playing the Hulk's tortured alter ego. Another plus was the casting of one of the nicest guys in show biz, that gentle giant Lou Ferrigno, who was the perfect choice to play the Green Goliath.

I learned a helluva lot about TV from Ken Johnson during the many discussions we had about how to best adapt *The Incredible Hulk* to television. The success of that show, under Ken's direction, proves beyond any doubt how important it is to put creative projects in the hands of truly creative people.

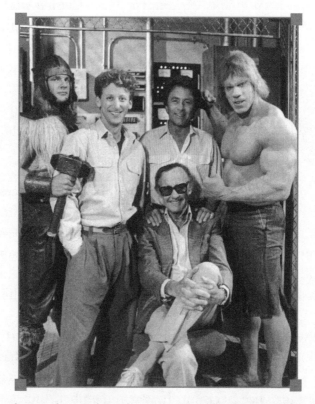

Bill Bixby taught me that when Lou Ferrigno (the Incredible Hulk) says "smile," mister, you better smile!

As The Incredible Hulk *thrilled both Stan's die-hard fans and ordinary television viewers alike, a pop music phenomenon was spreading across the nation. Decked out in space-age costumes and outlandish Kabuki-style makeup, the pop supergroup KISS was hitting the charts with screaming electric power ballads and selling out stadiums with over-the-top theatrics inspired by early-1970s "glam rock." Lead singer Gene Simmons was an enormous fan of Stan's work, which paved the way for one of the stranger projects in Stan's career.*

Of the many unusual experiences I had promoting our characters and books, something transpired while working with the musical group KISS that I'll never forget. It started with a publicity stunt while we were preparing to launch our *KISS* comicbook.

The idea was to take the group to the plant in Buffalo where our magazines were printed. Once there, the guys would go to the vat, or whatever you call it, where the red ink was kept. Then—and this is the truly incredible part—it had been arranged that each member of the group would prick one of his fingers with a pin. Next, all four of them would hold their fingers over the vat of red ink so that a few drops of blood, from each of them, would fall into the vat and mix with the ink. By doing that, they could claim that the ink used in printing every single copy of their magazine contained some portion of the actual blood of the members of KISS!

I guess there are no limits to what publicity people can dream up. And there I was, a part of the whole outlandish thing. But there's one other thing about that incredible affair that I can't get out of my mind.

The group chartered a plane for the trip to Buffalo and I went along with them. When we landed, wouldja believe there was actually a police escort waiting for us? All arranged by some public relations genius, I guess. The one thing that stuck in my mind is when we were driving in a limo, following the police on motorcycles with their red, white, and blue lights flashing. There were cops at the street corners holding up traffic while we passed by like some sort of presidential motorcade. All I could think of was that there were probably doctors on their way to see patients, mothers on the way to pick up their kids at school, people rushing to work—and all of them had to wait while these four guys from KISS were rushed to a printer to put a few drops of their blood into the red ink so that kids would feel they were getting KISS blood in their comicbook magazine.

Yep, thought I, that really says a lot about the society we live in!

By the end of the 1970s, comicbooks were so popular among both the old fans and the still-burgeoning collectors' market that stores specializing in comicbooks opened in neighborhoods throughout the country. In the comicbook trade, this distribution channel was called "direct sales," as opposed to the normal distribution system of a distributor bringing comicbooks to the usual, general magazine outlets.

Spotting a new, booming market, Marvel actively focused on this sector, hiring Carol Kalish to promote and place direct sales. Ultimately, she was able to increase Marvel sales by an additional 428,000 books a month. Pleased with these results, Marvel would find itself relying increasingly on direct sales in the years to come.

One of the best things about direct sales was the fact that the comicbook store owners were Marvel's most effective salespeople. Stan felt he had a good product, but at convenience stores or newsstands, it was lost among hundreds of other items. In contrast, the buyers who walk into a comicbook store are already pre-sold. They come in with the intention of buying a comicbook. The question is not will they buy a comic, but how many and which ones. Since Marvel's stable of superheroes was the most popular of all, it wasn't difficult to sell the comicbook store owner on the product and on buying multiple copies of each issue.

Although Stan personally had nothing to do with the distribu-

tion of the magazines, he became aware that Marvel had begun publishing comicbooks exclusively for the direct sales market, which gave the store owners still another reason to promote the company that was giving them an exclusive product that couldn't be purchased anywhere else. Marvel helped the dealers and the dealers reciprocated. It seemed to be a powerful strategy.

Speaking of strategy, it's the best way to describe how Stan made one of the most important moves of his life.

Mr. Marvel Becomes Joe Hollywood

As the 1970s drew to a close, Stan was spending an increasing amount of time in Los Angeles, trying to develop films in which Marvel characters would appear, as well as developing comicbooks based on Hollywood films. In 1977, for example, Marvel secured licensing for a six-episode series of comicbooks based on Star Wars; *a series which eventually sold more than a million copies and was so successful that Marvel had to rerun the presses twice to keep up with the demand.*

All this time, Stan was shuttling back and forth between New York and Hollywood so often that he felt it no longer made sense for Joanie and him to live in New York. Moreover, Stan was in the mood for a mid-career change. While he enjoyed his comicbook work in New York, Marvel's ventures into animation led him to ponder the new creative possibilities that the film world might open to him. From his early days of thrilling to action films in his youth, Stan had never lost his enduring fascination with Hollywood, the dream factory.

So, due to some clever strategizing on Stan's part, the Lees finally moved west in 1980 and Stan became the creative head of Marvel Productions in Hollywood.

In the past, whenever I visited Los Angeles I felt as though I had come to Nirvana. The indescribably beautiful weather, the mind-

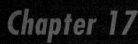

boggling scenery with mountains in the background and the ocean a stone's throw away, the wide avenues, the sprawling movie studios, trees, gardens, and flowers everywhere, and most exciting of all, the ability to drive a convertible with its top down twelve months a year. I wanted it. I wanted to live in L.A. I had to find a way.

Since we were now involved in animated cartoon versions of our characters, I hit upon the perfect plan. I told the gang at Marvel that we should be running our own animation studio instead of farming out the work to others. And, since there were now other people who could handle the comics, and since I was such a loyal and devoted employee, I would volunteer to unselfishly uproot my family and myself and move to Los Angeles to help set up such a studio for the good of the company, especially since we had an editor as competent as "Titanic" Tom DeFalco to keep a firm grip on things in the bullpen. Tom had written and edited so many of our top titles that I was certain he'd be the perfect man to handle the job.

By the time I finished relating my impassioned offer there wasn't a dry eye in the office. Everyone was impressed with my noble, self-sacrificing gesture, and so the lively little Lee ménage gleefully headed west.

Well, actually, most of the glee was on my part. Even to this day, neither my wife nor my daughter have really stopped missing New York. But valiant little troupers that they are, they've endured the rigors of life on a lovely hilltop, caressed by gentle breezes wafting through an evergreen garden as, from the terraces of each of their homes, they look down on the myriad of sparkling lights in the sprawling city below. Yep, they've learned to rough it with the best of 'em.

Luckily, Joanie had something else to keep her busy. One day, out of the blue, she told Stan she'd like to write a novel. Stan obligingly gave her a ream of paper and a few sharpened pencils and promptly forgot about it. A few months later Joanie handed him a large stack of pages and asked him to submit them to an agent. Dutiful husband that he was, Stan informed her that relatively few manuscripts are submitted in handwritten form. He hired someone to type it for her and sent it to Jonathan Dolger, an agent whom he had known when Jonathan was an editor at Simon & Schuster. In fact, it was Jonathan who had bought Stan's Origins of Marvel Comics and all the subsequent titles in that series. Stan enclosed a note asking Jonathan to be merciful with his critique because Joanie, who had never written anything professionally before, had spent months writing her book.

Imagine Stan's surprise, and Joanie's elation, when Jonathan wrote back a few days later saying that the book was beautifully written and he was sure he could sell it—which he did, to Dell Books, a short time later. It was published as a lead paperback entitled The Pleasure Palace, *and Joanie was now a professional novelist. She is finishing her second novel even as these words are being written.*

When we first arrived in L.A., we took a year's lease in a high-rise condo in Westwood, adjacent to Beverly Hills, from which I attempted to get the lay of the land before deciding where we'd want to drop anchor permanently. That was when I witnessed my first typical Los Angeles disaster.

One day, from our windows in the condo, we saw a huge fire in the hills above the Sunset Strip. It was a scary affair, with helicopters, one after the other, dropping tons of water, trying to save the homes below as fire engines raced frantically through the streets with their sirens going full blast. It was like a scene in a disaster movie. I remember saying to Joan, "Why would anyone buy a house in a wooded area like that which is so vulnerable to fire?"

Well, months later, we finally decided on the home we wanted

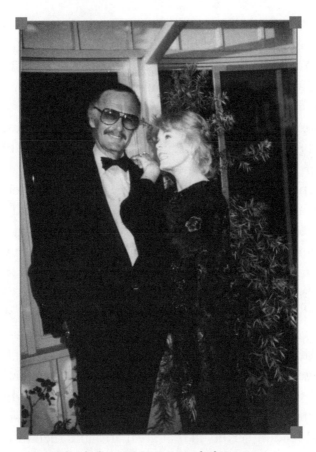

Why fight it? Joanie's mad about me!

to buy. Where was it located? I'll give you one guess. In that very same area—a heavily-wooded little paradise above the Sunset Strip!

As yet, our house is still unburned, but there was one event that really shook us up.

The day Joanie and I were to move into our first house in California was a big day for us. I bought a bottle of champagne and gallantly carried her over the threshold, feeling overwhelmingly triumphant and romantic. Just as we were about to drink a toast to each other on the terrace, with the city at our feet below, we heard music coming from the small guest house on the property. Since it was too much to expect that the guest house itself was welcoming us in its own unique way, we thought it best to investigate. That's when the shock set in.

There was a guy living there, right in our guest house. When I suggested that we weren't running a motel, he said he had no intention of leaving. He claimed he had a one-year lease entitling him to remain there, given to him by the previous owner.

So much for the romantic episode Joanie and I had planned.

No need to lay all the gory details on you. We had to call the police, bring in a lawyer, and threaten the real estate agent until we finally managed to divest ourselves of "our tenant." It was a truly upsetting situation but every cloud has a silver lining. That little episode did enable me to fill up a few more paragraphs in this book.

But that wasn't my only traumatic situation at that time.

Marvel Productions, as we called our new animation company, had set up a studio in a great little one-story building in Van Nuys, centered around a sun-filled atrium. I enjoyed sitting outdoors and reading scripts in that great area and then discussing all our projects with David DePatie of *Pink Panther* fame, whom we hired to run the studio for us and who, with his lovely wife, Marcia, soon became two of our closest friends.

I also kept dozens of videotapes of the many TV interviews and lectures I had done over the years in one of the storerooms in the studio. But most important of all was a magnificent bust of Joanie that had been done by Stanley Sawyer, an old friend from Long Island. I had kept that bust on the window ledge of every office I had had, for at least twenty years. It was the centerpiece of my office decor at Marvel Productions and I loved looking at it every day, until—

I received a phone call. "The studio has burned down." It was as sudden and unexpected as that. It had happened at night, when everyone was gone. The fire department suspected arson, possibly some disgruntled ex-employee, although they never found the arsonist. Overnight, I had not only lost all my videotapes, but that priceless bust of Joanie. I consoled myself with the fact that no lives were lost and no one had been injured, and luckily I still have the original at home with me.

While Hollywood was a whole different world from the New York where Stan had spent his entire life, it retained some of the same features. In New York, Stan had lived two lives, one his real life in Long Island and Manhattan, and the other his fantasy life in the World of Comics. Moving to sunny Los Angeles, Stan found himself once again living in a fantasy world, albeit a somewhat different type and on a much larger scale.

Given his reputation among the entertainment world's creative elite, a large portion of whom had grown up marveling at his creations, Stan was flattered when Hollywood welcomed him with open arms. Nevertheless, the émigré comicbook caliph found that dealing with the corporate side of Hollywood was ultimately not that much different from dealing with the suits in New York.

I'll never forget my first encounter, in 1981, with a network VP to whom I was pitching an idea for an animated series. Since it was our first meeting she acted as though she really wanted to get to know me, to learn how I felt about Saturday morning cartoons. I was genuinely pleased when she asked for my opinion of the cartoons appearing on network TV at the time.

Trying to be as candid as possible, I told her I thought most cartoons were beautifully drawn and well animated. The only thing I couldn't understand, said I, sincerely trying to be helpful, was why the stories themselves were, for the most part, so unintelligent, with characters speaking in cartoon-speak rather than with real dialogue.

If you shut your eyes, I told her, and turned on the TV, you could always tell when a cartoon series was playing because the dialogue would be so unnatural and "cartoony-sounding."

At that point, she looked me straight in the eye and said, "We don't want our series to consist of talking heads."

Still thinking I had a chance of reaching her, I replied, "I'm not advocating 'talking heads,' or using more dialogue. I'm only suggesting that whatever dialogue you use be better written."

I was hoping for a chance to give her some concrete examples. But she immediately snapped back, "We're not looking for talking heads."

It was like a scene from *Alice in Wonderland*. I felt I was at a mad tea party. No matter what I said, her only retort was, "We don't want talking heads."

However, I did learn a lesson. I realized that when some executives ask what you think about anything, it's purely a rhetorical question.

She repeated the talking heads bit three or four more times and, since I don't need a bridge to fall on me, I eventually gave up; nor did I ever pitch her another show.

When I related that little incident to my friend David De-Patie, he simply smiled and told me, "Welcome to Hollywood."

The year 1986 was marked by at least two notable events in Stan's life, a birthday and another change in company ownership. The birthday was the official twenty-fifth anniversary of Marvel Comics, after its earlier years as Timely and Atlas Comics. The new company ownership came when Cadence sold Marvel yet again, this time to New World, which had been a Roger Corman film company but was now owned by cochairmen Larry Kuppin and Harry Sloane, with Robert Rehme as CEO. New World saw Marvel, its creative properties, its animation division, and all of its talent as a great match with their television production company and their plans for the future.

One thing that never sat well with Stan was the fact that Sheldon Feinberg had given shares of Marvel to about a dozen of his executives, all of them in the business area, such as his lawyers, accountants, and assorted vice presidents, but nothing went to any creative people such as Stan. So when the company was sold once again, many people who had little or nothing to do with Marvel's success ended up with large sums of money while Stan was given a handshake. He felt there was a lesson to be learned from all that, though he was never quite sure what it was.

But, once again, his ability not to dwell on the past served him well. A new chapter was about to open in his life and Stan was eager to face it.

Whenever new management takes over a company, it's always a time of trepidation for the employees. How will things change? Will the changes affect my salary, my job duties, my benefits? Will I like the new people? Will they like me? In fact, will they want to keep me on at all?

I had been through this so many times, with so many changes of ownership and management, that I was pretty inured to it by now. Besides, I had a feeling that Joanie would welcome it if I told her I had finally left Marvel and would now try to join the real world. But, like everyone else, I was still eager to see what was going to happen now that we were a New World company. No matter what the result would be, I knew it would be a change and that was fine with me. I hate being in a rut. I've always loved change.

The big day finally came. The cochairmen of New World, together with Bob Rehme and their board of directors, were gathered in the big conference room and meeting with the company's executives, one by one. Finally, it was my turn to be led into the lions' den.

I'll never forget the first moment when I walked in. A few of the directors stood up and came over to me, enthusiastically shaking my hand and asking if I'd autograph some comicbooks for their children. A couple of them actually wanted my autograph for themselves. At that moment I suspected they might be inclined to keep me on.

I liked the guys at New World, and I especially liked, and still like, Bob Rehme. To me, he was what a genuine Hollywood executive should be. He was articulate, energetic, knowledgeable, and straight-talking. One man like Bob can make up for a half-dozen phonies that one might meet along the way.

Needless to say, my position at New World seemed secure. I left the animation studio and moved to the New World headquarters building in Westwood where I ended up with a most impressive office and my own adjacent conference room. I decided that I was liking show biz better and better.

It was an interesting time for me. Instead of concentrating on animation, I was now involved with movies and television as well. But, as always, there were of course some frustrations.

Despite the fact that it had been "in development" for almost a dozen years, *Spider-Man* was still no closer to reaching the big screen. We did manage to produce a couple of movies based on other Marvel characters, *Captain America* and *The Punisher,* but they were both low-budget productions and did little to enhance the Marvel image.

Meanwhile, Joanie and I were enjoying life in Tinseltown. We attended some colorful parties, met some interesting celebrities, and went to a gallery exhibition of our daughter's paintings that made us feel quite proud. In case I forgot to mention it, our daughter Joanie is not only beautiful but incredibly talented.

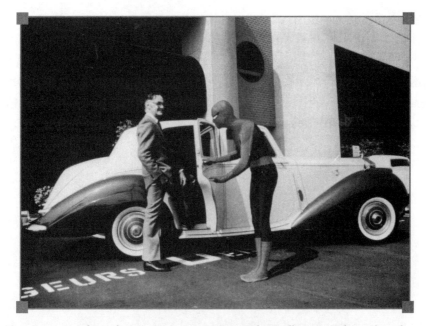

This was one of my favorite cars, a 1950 "Baby Rolls." Note how this photo depicts my most endearing quality—an admirable lack of ostentation.

I guess there really is a great case to be made for genetics. My brother Larry and I both gravitated toward art and writing, with Larry leaning more heavily on art and me concentrating more on the writing. As for young Joanie, she has totally inherited the same love for all things creative that her mother and I share. I won't even mention what a terrific actress she is or what great lyrics she writes because you might suspect that I, who am obviously the very soul of modesty, might be bragging just a tad.

As an artist, young Joanie has just one strange little quirk—she's never willing to sell her paintings. Too bad she didn't inherit some of her father's greed. People often ask to buy one but J.C. always manages to find some excuse not to sell them. Personally, I wish she would sell some because quite a few of them are huge and, not only does she keep them in her own house, but we've been storing a zillion canvases all over our home, too. Oh well, it could be worse; she could be sculpting dinosaurs.

Lately, she's been designing jewelry, much of it beaded. Happily, unlike her paintings, she's been willing to part with these new creations and we're all delighted that they seem to be selling at a fast clip. Just my luck—she won't let go of the large paintings that

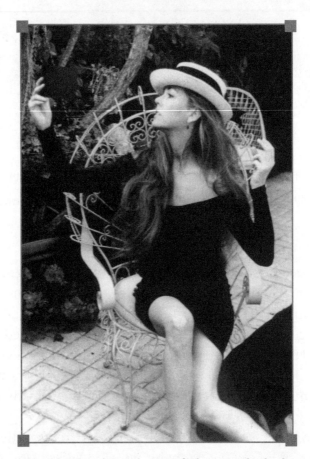

Like mother, like daughter. The art of photography had certainly peaked with this exquisite example of exotic elegance from the halcyon modeling days of J. C. Lee. Told with stunning objectivity by her proud pop!

take up so much room in both our houses, but the jewelry, which would be no trouble for us to store—those pieces go out as fast as she designs them.

Sometimes I get the feeling that my wife and daughter are the real talents in our little family and I'm just the front guy. But, hey, I can deal with that.

Speaking of talent, I've got to tell you about my cousin Mel Stuart. Being a world-class name-dropper, I loved telling people that Mel was my cousin because he's the guy who directed the legendary movie *Willy Wonka & the Chocolate Factory*. He moved to L.A. long before I did but we've since become fast friends. He now specializes in impressive TV documentaries and is one of the most knowledgeable guys I know. But that's not the story I wanna tell you. We hated each other when we first met.

It was years ago in New York. I was master of my tiny domain at Marvel Comics and he was a big Hollywood player who came to see me. We had never been close at that time. In fact, I had to wrack my brain to remember who Mel Stuart was. It developed that he was interested in having me do a comicbook about Neil Diamond, for some reason or other.

I'm embarrassed to admit this, but at that time I just vaguely knew the name Neil Diamond. I asked how much he'd pay Marvel for us to produce such a book.

Mel grew indignant, telling me that we would have to pay Diamond for the privilege of doing a comic about him.

One thing led to another, with Mel accusing me of being a cretin for not acknowledging how big a name Neil Diamond was, while I told him to high-tail it back to Hollywood and to remember that Marvel Comics was bigger than any cockamamie singer.

These days, we laugh about that long-ago session almost every time we get together. With an episode like that behind us, I think it's a real coup that we ended up becoming fast friends.

And I still say Marvel is bigger than any singer.

It's fortunate for Stan that he likes change and has the ability to adapt to it easily, because another major shift in his career was about to occur.

One morning, as the mist cleared off the East River, Ronald Perelman had Marvel in his crosshairs. Perelman's friends said he was just doing what he had been doing for the previous nine years, sewing together a patchwork conglomerate that included Revlon cosmetics, along with MacAndrews & Forbes (America's largest producer of licorice extract), Technicolor (the company responsible for producing the color in Hollywood films), Pantry Pride (a grocery store chain), and a random assortment of other companies. Marvel, the company whose creative output Stan had led for decades, was to be next.

In 1988, Perelman acquired both Marvel Comics and New World Entertainment. To further expand Marvel's presence in film and television, he organized a new company called Marvel Films and tapped Stan to head that operation.

What I always tried to do with Marvel was make the company very visible and creative, and I guess that visibility and creativity was part of what attracted Ron Perelman.

When Ron took over, I was excited by the prospect that, for the first time, Marvel would be owned by a very wealthy man who headed a very wealthy conglomerate. I hoped it would give us as much financial clout as our main rival, DC Comics, which was owned by Warner Bros.

I've always seemed to be lucky at first meetings. Certainly the one I had with the New World board had gone splendidly. Now I was due to meet the man who would run things for Ron Perelman at Marvel, one of the most elegant dressers in the business, a very private, yet amiable Southern gentleman named Bill Bevins.

As usual, I had no idea what to expect when I walked into Bill's office for the first time. We exchanged pleasantries for a few minutes and then, unexpectedly, he asked what my annual income was at Marvel. After I told him, he looked at me thoughtfully for a minute or two and then, in the calmest, most matter-of-fact way, he told me that henceforth I'd be earning approximately triple that amount.

At first I wasn't sure I had heard him correctly, but was reluctant to ask him to repeat what he had said, in case he'd change his mind. When I got home and told Joanie what had transpired, we spent quite a while trying to figure out what he must have really said—what could have sounded like "triple"? We couldn't think of

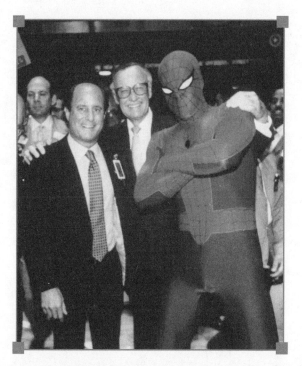

The New York Stock Exchange on the day Marvel went public.
I was tempted to offer Ron Perelman some financial advice,
but hey, I was busy with my comicbooks.

anything so we decided to wait until pay day and see what the actual payment would be.

The big day arrived. I received my check. It was almost triple the usual amount!

I wouldn't care if people told me that Bill Bevins is an ax murderer—I love the guy!

The Catastrophic Collecting Craze

So Stan and Marvel were now part of the Perelman empire and everything seemed to be rolling along smoothly. Marvel was still numero uno in comics, and Stan was becoming part of the movie and TV establishment.

As the days went by, nobody was quite prepared for the next surprising development that was about to affect Marvel Comics as well as the entire comicbook industry.

It's still hard to believe. Probably the first time in history that an entire industry hit bottom because of increased customer demand.

Even now, as I think back on it, the end result was motivated by greed, plain and simple, as well as a measure of stupidity on the part of everyone concerned, the publishers and the fans alike.

What happened was, the fans one day learned that there was money in collecting comics. Major auction galleries such as Sotheby's and Christie's began auctioning off old comicbooks and original comicbook art at hitherto unimaginable prices. A copy of the origin issue of *Spider-Man, Superman,* or *Batman,* for example, could bring prices in the tens of thousands. Even obscure titles that had become hard to find were selling for hundreds and sometimes thousands of dollars.

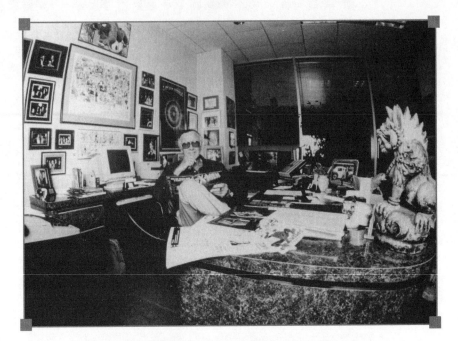

This was my all-time favorite office, when Marvel was
part of New World. I put lots of papers on my desk
so I'd look busy, but no one was fooled.

To feed the flames of fandom's frenzy even further, newspapers and magazines started writing articles that touted the fact that comicbooks were better investments than stocks because their rate of appreciation was so much higher.

Before long, average comicbook readers became avid collectors. Rather than buy one copy of a favorite issue, they would buy a dozen or more copies, one to read and the others to save, keeping them in mint condition, hoping to sell them for many times the cover price in the near future.

Naturally, the publishers doubled and tripled their print orders in order to accommodate fandom's feeding frenzy and to cash in for themselves. Suddenly, comicbook companies were printing and selling more copies per month than they had ever dreamed they could. The market had become a publishing paradise. Everyone was racing along the new path to instant riches—collecting comicbooks. Nobody took the time to think about how the whole, unnatural system was bound to end.

Marvel, and other companies as well, even resorted to such tactics as having two printings of the same magazine, one with one cover and the other with a different cover, knowing that the rabid fans would buy copies of each so as to have complete sets which always brought a premium when sold. In that way, the publishers could sell twice as many copies of the same issue.

Another device was to print "collectors" covers with special ink or holograms, anything to make the magazine seem like it would bring a premium when sold at auction later on.

Naturally, it couldn't go on. The bubble had to burst.

It happened when the collectors finally ran out of money. They simply couldn't afford to buy all the magazines that were being poured into the market. And so, eager to finally realize a profit on their investment, fans all over the country, if not the world, began trying to sell some of the many issues they had been buying and hoarding.

That's when the shock hit them. They found that their copies were a glut on the market. There were just too many of them.

At last, the truth slowly began to sink in—old comicbooks were valuable because they were rare. The new titles that readers had so greedily gobbled up were a dime a dozen; everybody already owned them. Far from being rare, they were all over the place. Nobody will pay a premium price for something that's in plentiful supply.

Not only were the readers caught with many worthless comics on their hands, but the publishers, too, took a financial bath by having overprinted so many more comicbooks than they could possibly sell.

Also, because they had stocked too many books themselves, the owners of many comicbook stores ended up unable to pay for all the copies that were cluttering up their shelves. Consequently, a few thousand retail stores went belly-up, leaving the publishers with too few outlets for their product. Where there had once been more than six thousand comicbook stores in the United States alone, there were now about two thousand. You don't have to be an Einstein to figure—the fewer comicbook stores you have, the fewer comics will be sold.

It turned into a real debacle. From an artificial sales high, the industry sank to a realistic, money-losing low. Comicbooks were in trouble once again.

In the summer of 1993, Marvel began to form "strategic alliances." In such a scenario, two enterprises get together to create a third operation, creating synergy, which is supposed to be better than either of the original two alone. Thus, Marvel Entertainment Group, Inc., and ToyBiz, Inc., joined to form a new company called ToyBiz, which would be licensed to make action figures and other toys based on Marvel's heroes and other characters. ToyBiz was run by Ike Perlmutter and Avi Arad. The Marvel people saw little or nothing of Perlmutter, who kept to himself at the toy company's headquarters, but Arad, a well-known toy designer, who had created toys for Mattel, Hasbro, and similar companies, soon became a hands-on executive at Marvel.

Perelman also bought the famous bubble-gum company, Fleer, maker of Dubble Bubble gum. Fleer was big in the sports trading-card business. The connections were all part of a global plan under which the new company, ToyBiz, hoped to sell merchandise to some thirty foreign countries—a promising venture.

Unfortunately, Marvel's streak of bad luck continued. The 1994 baseball strike turned mobs of fans against the sport and robbed them of any incentive to buy, collect, or trade Fleer's baseball cards. When Marvel endeavored to cut costs by firing talented members of its creative staff, it drove many of them to the competition.

Like sharks that come rushing for the kill when they smell blood, corporate raiders came swarming. That's when Carl Icahn entered the picture. One of the sharpest corporate raiders ever, he received $34 million for seizing complete control of TWA and turning it from a public company into one which was privately held— by Carl Icahn. In the mid-1990s, Icahn went after Marvel, and he and Perelman were soon locked in a battle for control of the company.

I was, of course, living in Los Angeles at the time, and all I knew about the Perelman/Icahn battle was what I heard from the gang in New York or what I'd read in the papers. I found it exciting, sort of like reading a comicbook about a couple of superpowered titans who were battling to control a galaxy. If they flew spaceships it could have been *Star Wars*. Some of their financial maneuvers— the few I was able to understand—were, to me, truly fantastic— and that's coming from a guy who had made characters fly through the air, burst into flame, shatter steel doors, and crawl up tall buildings.

Perelman and his bankers were outraged at Icahn's demands and had Marvel file for Chapter 11 bankruptcy. This move allowed Perelman to restructure the company while keeping its assets away from such creditors as Icahn and the other bondholders. From his Manhattan offices, Icahn fumed in an interview, "A caretaker has no right to take away ownership of a home, especially after he damages the property." In May of 1997, Icahn went to court and convinced a federal judge to hand over control of the company to the bondholders led by Icahn.

So, at the end of May 1997, we had a new boss, Carl Icahn, who installed Joe Calamari to run things at Marvel. I was pretty much okay with that, because Joe and I were friends. He had been a VP at Marvel Comics in the past and was one of the few execs who really knew something about comicbooks. He was also a bright, hard-working dynamo of a guy, and, even though I was doing my own thing in Los Angeles, I looked forward to things picking up under his management.

But Joe's reign turned out to be a short one. Just when it looked as though Carl Icahn was firmly in the driver's seat, the ToyBiz people made an end run around him and won control of the company for themselves. Within hours Joe was gone and Avi Arad was once again the man in charge.

Even though he was a crack businessman, Avi preferred the creative end of the business and, luckily, he was good at it. He soon turned his attention to the movie, TV, and animation part of Marvel, just as he and I had done months earlier, creating cartoon shows and pitching movies and TV projects to the studios and networks. It was fun, exciting, and an education for us both. Avi was energetic and knowledgeable, and had a great creative flair. I enjoyed working with him.

But all good things eventually come to an end. Finally, the biggest change of all in my career at Marvel took place. It was toward the end of 1998, while the company was still working its way through its bankruptcy. An announcement came down from on high—"All contracts will be terminated!"

Of course, I didn't for a minute think that edict included me. I had had a lifetime contract with Marvel for decades. I figured I'd be there until that far-off day when I'd be too weak to shout "Excelsior!" Marvel was as much my home as the house that Joanie and I shared. So I didn't give that announcement much thought.

I should have!

A few days later I had a call from Ike Perlmutter, the senior partner of the Perlmutter/Arad team, the one who supposedly made the business decisions, the one I had virtually no relationship with. He asked if I'd come to New York to see him.

In my almost unforgivable naiveté, I cheerfully flew east, thinking it was nice that he wanted to be friends.

Ike greeted me like a long-lost brother, telling me how important I was to him and the company and assuring me that I'd be making more money than ever from then on. I thought to myself, Gee, why did people tell me he's such a cold fish? He's one helluva nice guy. As you can see, I'm a very tough guy to impress.

Bottom line. I was offered a new contract. Not a lifetime contract as before, but for a period of two years. Not "more money than ever," but exactly half what I had been earning.

I wondered if Mr. Perlmutter had gone to the same school as Martin Goodman.

Well, look, a man who owns a company has the right to run it the way he wants to. But luckily, through the good offices of my friend, Joe Calamari, I had met a great lawyer named Arthur Lieberman. Without going into all the sordid details (you see enough of them in the countless courtroom dramas on TV), after a period of negotiation, I was again given the same lifetime arrangement that I'd had before, plus a salary that I felt was fair. Instead of my previous title of "chairman," I would be, now and forevermore, "chairman emeritus" of Marvel.

One of the best features of my new deal is the fact that it allows me to do any other work I choose, for anyone else, or even to form a company of my own, if I wish to. No matter what, I'll still be chairman emeritus of Marvel, which pleases the hell out of me because I'll always love that company, no matter who runs it. In fact, I still spend at least 10 percent of my time on Marvel projects, such as writing the *Spider-Man* newspaper strip, doing interviews, keeping up with fan mail, and, of course, writing an occasional script for one of our comics.

So, all is well with Marvel and me. Aided by their extremely competent new editor-in-chief, Joe Quesada, and the indescribably talented bullpen which Joe assembled, Ike and Avi seem to be doing a fine job of bringing the company back to its former glory.

As for Stan, his own life was about to become as wild and incredible as any of the stories he had ever written.

Almost a Tycoon

Let's start by going back a few years.

In the middle of the nineties a friend of mine named Larry Shultz one day reminded me that my contract allowed me to work on movies and TV apart from my duties at Marvel. He suggested that we form a two-man company and try our luck in show biz.

Since it's hard for me to say no to anything that sounds interesting, we formed Lee-Shultz Productions and immediately started to create concepts for movies and TV. Larry is an unusually talented guy, a scientific whiz who has made a bundle by selling various inventions of his, but also a good man with whom to kick ideas around. We hit it off well together and actually sold a screenplay named *Tomorrow* to 20th Century Fox. It hasn't yet been filmed but we live in hope.

We also came up with a number of television concepts and had a great time meeting with writers, directors, and producers, and forming strategic alliances that didn't go anywhere but gave us a lot of experience. Even today, some of the projects we started in the nineties are now being considered at various studios.

However, in 1988, something was about to happen that would take me away from those spare-time projects and propel me into a whole new world.

Not many people in their late seventies decide to start an entirely new career, but then, not many people are Stan Lee.

Even though he held the title "chairman emeritus," Stan realized that there was less and less for him to do at Marvel. The comics were produced at Marvel's New York offices, but he was living in Los Angeles. Sure, he could write an occasional story for the company, but it wasn't the same as when he himself had been in charge. In those days, he determined the type of strip to do, the page length of the strip, which artist to use, how he wanted the strip drawn, and how he wanted the cover to be designed. Everything had been under Stan's control. But now it was different. Now, whenever he would write a comicbook, he was like any other freelance writer, subject to the vision of the editor.

Luckily for Stan, he and the editors were all friends and he felt they were all highly competent. But it still wasn't the same as in the past. It didn't have the same excitement, the same feeling that he was in a position to break new ground with whatever he was creating.

As for Stan's involvement with Marvel's animation, movies, and TV projects, once Avi Arad had arrived on the scene, Avi was the one who began to make the decisions, the one who became the authoritative voice of Marvel. At first, Stan had accompanied him to all the creative meetings, giving his own advice and comments about stories and themes, functioning as part of the creative team. But, as time went on, Avi seemed to desire less and less of Stan's input.

To be fair, Stan thought Avi did quite well in his new task. Of course, he had a great ballpark to play in. It would be difficult not to do well when you controlled characters like the X-Men, Spider-Man, the Hulk, Daredevil, and so many additional heroes who had been popular for decades, and were offering them to studios that were hungry for proven characters that could be franchised. Yet, Stan felt that Avi handled his responsibilities with intelligence and dedication.

Stan also remembered that when he was running Marvel, he wouldn't have welcomed someone else second-guessing him. So he could understand that it was perfectly natural for Avi, who was now handling Marvel's entertainment projects, to prefer to do his job without any input from Stan.

It dawned on Stan that he was left with two choices. He could either live the life of an indolent retiree or find something new that would challenge him creatively. He felt he was as good or better a writer than ever and was still brimming with countless ideas for new characters and themes.

And that's where Peter Paul came in.

I had known Peter Paul, whose name sounded like a candy bar or the head of the Church, for about ten years. He first came to see me with Fabio, a client of his whose face and figure had graced countless paperback romance covers. It seems that Fabio had heard we might be doing a movie based on our character Thor, God of Thunder, and he was interested in trying for the part. Far as I was concerned he might have been great in the role; he certainly looked like Thor ought to look. But we weren't doing a Thor movie at that time, so that ended that.

Except it didn't end Peter Paul.

He called me later to ask if I'd consent to be an honoree at a prestigious affair he was throwing for his nonprofit Spirit of America Foundation. When he told me that he and Jimmy Stewart were the organizers of the affair and the guests would include Ronald Reagan and Helen Hayes, I had accepted almost before he finished talking.

When I asked why I, of all people, was chosen to receive a Spirit of America award, Peter said it was because of all I had done for young people, helping to foster literacy and the best ideals of America. Hey, I wasn't about to argue with that.

The evening came off beautifully. Joanie and I were seated at a table right next to Ronald Reagan, who had left the presidency a short time before. I'll never forget part of my conversation with him. I was desperately thinking, What do you say to an ex-president? You see, it may come as a surprise, but I didn't number very many heads of state among my closest friends.

Finally, I took a deep breath and said, "Mr. President, I imagine you must be tremendously relieved to be a civilian again and finally be free of all those heavy cares and responsibilities." It was the sort of remark that would be easy to answer with a polite nod as he'd continue eating. But no! He looked at me with his eyes wide and sparkling, with enthusiasm gushing out of every pore as he replied, "Oh, no! I *loved* being president!" It was the most natural, unstudied, spontaneous reaction ever from a man who obviously *had* loved being president. I'll never forget that moment.

But, getting back to Peter Paul. He was always arranging for me to meet prominent people. He proved to be a man who managed to gain access to some of the biggest names in Hollywood and in politics. Through Peter, over the years I have met, among many others, the president of Poland, Tony Curtis, Whoopi Goldberg, Ginger Rogers, Al Gore, Muhammad Ali, Governor Gray Davis, Bill and Hillary Clinton, and received a Certificate of Appreciation from then-mayor Tom Bradley on behalf of the City of Los Angeles for something or other.

Peter told me he had previously been an international lawyer and showed me signed photographs from various Supreme Court justices and congressmen. I'm a guy who's impressed with someone who knows how to talk to headwaiters, so you can imagine how impressed I was with Peter Paul.

And so we return to my wondering what I'd do with the rest of my life after Avi had taken over the entertainment part of Marvel's business.

Peter approached me one day, I think it was in 1998, and said, "Let's form a company." I started to laugh, because it reminded me

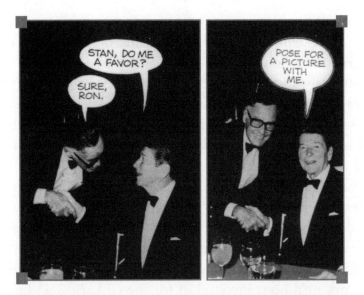

One of my favorite things—putting words in people's mouths.
Ron probably was really just asking me for political advice.

of those old Judy Garland/Mickey Rooney movies where the kids say, "Let's put on a show." But Peter was serious. He said, "The Internet's the big thing now, and someone like you can create all sorts of entertainment for the Web."

When I told him I didn't know squat about forming companies, he told me not to worry about it because he did. Within a few months, under his aegis, "Stan Lee Media" was born. Peter convinced me to take the title "chairman," saying that he'd remain behind the scenes to handle the managerial part.

Next thing I knew, he had found a way to take us public. I'm still not sure how he did it, but there we were on the stock exchange! He arranged for each of us to have more than 6 million shares of stock, which sounded awfully impressive to me although the stock had little or no value at that time. He also told me that, as chairman of a public company, I'd have to give up all outside work, including my work with Larry Shultz, and devote my full time to Stan Lee Media. So I did.

My first project was to dream up a group of characters and themes for animated episodes on our Web site. We called them "webisodes," of course. After hiring a team of terrific artists, I felt like I was back in those exciting early days of Marvel. Stan Lee Media was on its way.

Later I learned that we had to have a board of directors, a chief executive officer, and all the things a public company needs. I asked Peter why he didn't want the title of president or CEO of our company, since he was running it anyway. He told me he had done time years ago when he was about twenty. It had to do with work he'd been involved in for the CIA. He said he'd been framed by Communist sympathizers and served a small sentence rather than reveal CIA secrets, or something of that sort. Having been a convicted felon, he said he couldn't officially be running our public company nor could he sit on the board—but he'd be an advisor.

Being a trusting guy, I accepted his story at face value and concentrated on creating the best products I could for our company.

Things were great for the first year. We kept adding to our staff until we had over 150 employees. We were written about in trade publications as one of the most successful and promising Internet companies. At one time I was told my stock was worth in the neighborhood of $90 million! Unfortunately, I learned it couldn't be sold for a couple of years, but that was okay with me. I figured by then it would be worth a billion! Here's a tip—never come to me for financial advice.

One thing I have to mention is the staff I assembled. I thought I'd never be able to find artists as good as the ones I'd worked with back in New York. Well, I was wrong. Before long, to produce our animated webisodes, I had a new bullpen consisting of Will Meugniot, Aaron Soud, Ruben Martinez, Russ Heath, and Anthony Winn. It would take another complete book for me to tell you what great artists these guys were, and what a joy they were to work with. That's one area where I feel I've been extremely lucky; I've always managed to end up working with incredibly talented people.

Just before the bubble burst, Peter even organized a farewell party for Bill Clinton at the end of the year 2000. Even there he had an ulterior motive. He was hoping we could persuade him to join our board of directors after he left office.

Stan tells a very amusing story about his wife and Hillary Clinton. When he first met the ex-First Lady, he lightheartedly introduced Joanie to her as his trophy wife, which brought a big smile from Hillary. A few weeks later, at a fund-raising cocktail party, Stan and Joanie again ran into Hillary Clinton. Not sure whether she would remember them, Stan started to make a new introduction when Hillary interrupted him by saying, with a warm smile, "Hello, Stan. How are you and your trophy wife?" You can imagine how that feat of memory must have impressed a man who admittedly has trouble recalling what he ate for breakfast.

The farewell party that Peter Paul organized for Bill Clinton was one of the biggest bashes ever, with a host of Hollywood luminaries performing. I thought it just didn't get any better than that.

I was right. It didn't. It got worse.

Within a matter of weeks, Stan learned that Stan Lee Media couldn't meet its payroll. The company was compelled to go into bankruptcy. But that wasn't the worst of it.

The SEC, the FBI, and the Justice Department began to investi-

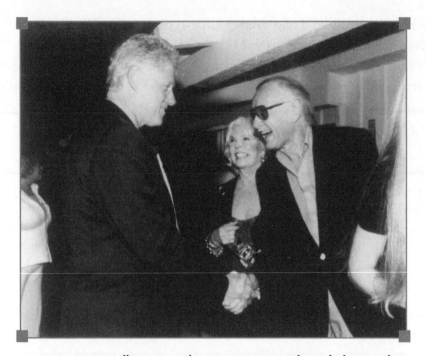

Every picture tells a story. This one proves conclusively how cool
and laid-back Joanie and I are when meeting celebrities.

gate certain "irregularities" in the company's management and fi-
nances. Suddenly, Peter Paul became the focus of the investigation.

One day, Stan was amazed to learn that Peter, his wife, and his
children had left the country and gone to Brazil, where Peter was re-
puted to have some of his own business interests. That was the last
Stan heard from him.

At the time of this writing, Paul has been arrested and is in jail
somewhere in Brazil. To say that it was a shock to Stan would be the
understatement of the year. He had trusted Peter implicitly.

Even now, I can't believe the whole thing happened. So many people, including myself, have been hurt.

Next to my wife and daughter, the things I've always treasured most have been my relationships with people. So I try to tell my-self—to have one go bad out of so very many isn't too shabby a record. Still, no platitude will ever repair the harm that's been done, to me and countless others. But one thing's for sure—

I'll never be so stupidly trusting again.

From Spidey to Superman

The unhappy episode with Stan Lee Media might have really gotten me down if it weren't for the fact that I've always been lucky enough to have a lot of things to work on, and as long as I can keep busy it saves me from dwelling too much on the past.

Also, I'm tremendously excited about all the movies that Marvel has, both in production and in development. Of course, the one thing everyone wants to ask me about is the *Spider-Man* film. Boy, if only they knew the agonizing, inside story about why it took so long to get that movie made.

Over the years, a lot of people had told Stan that Spider-Man *was the hottest property in Hollywood, and that a* Spider-Man *epic would be the movie event of the year. The only problem was figuring out who had the right to film it. The battle to settle that question had dragged on for seven years, involving five lawsuits over eighteen agreements. At one point, three studios claimed to have the right to make the* Spider-Man *feature film.*

It started in 1975, when Menahem Golan, a prolific independent filmmaker who specialized in low-budget Chuck Norris and Charles Bronson type movies, bought a five-year option from Marvel, giving him the right to produce a Spider-Man *movie. In trying* to develop the Spider-Man *movie, Golan went through four years and ten scripts before he thought he was ready, but by then he was out of money and his Cannon Films was eventually gobbled up by Pathé Communications, which was run by a suspect Italian promoter who later had to flee the United States to escape a warrant for his arrest.*

Golan later got Cannon Films back and changed its name to 21st Century Films. He renegotiated his deal with Marvel to give him time beyond the deadline of August 1990 to make Spider-Man. *Golan began raising the millions he thought he needed by selling off subsidiary rights to* Spider-Man *before the movie was even made. He sold the foreign distribution rights for various countries, television rights to Viacom, and home video rights to Columbia Tri-Star. In short, he sold practically everything one could sell of* Spider-Man *except the webbing and the U.S. distribution rights.*

Golan then met with the executives of Carolco, an independent film company that was in clover after its hits Aliens *and* The Terminator. *In 1990, Golan sold the* Spider-Man *package to Carolco for $5 million and a producer credit on the film. In 1991, Carolco spent another $3 million hiring James Cameron—at that time famous for having directed* Aliens, The Terminator, *and* Terminator 2*—to write the script.*

I had always been a great fan of Jim Cameron's and was in puppy heaven when I learned he might be the one to write and direct the web-slinger's movie. I had a number of meetings with Jim, and the more we spoke the more my confidence in him grew.

Finally, I think it was in 1993, I received a fifty-seven-page document from Jim marked "Eyes Only: Not for Duplication." It was like getting a secret dispatch from the CIA. I was thrilled. While it wasn't the full script, it was the most detailed, thoroughly documented treatment for a big budget movie I'd ever seen. As I greedily pored over page after page, I could see each scene unfolding in my imagination. I said to myself, At last—we're there! But I still had a lot to learn about the booby traps in Hollywood film-making.

While the Spider-Man *project was being developed at Carolco, Golan was having an ego attack because in all the advance publicity his name was never mentioned as "producer." The only name Golan kept seeing connected with the movie was the more marketable one of James Cameron.*

Carolco executive Lynwood Spinks reluctantly explained to Golan that in their eagerness to sign James Cameron to do the script, Carolco had taken a copy of his Terminator *contract and substituted the name* Spider-Man *throughout it. This particular contract gave Cameron final say on every credit given in the picture. Cameron refused to give Golan producer credit even if Carolco's deal had promised him that. In April 1993, Golan sued to set aside the contract, a move that opened a floodgate of lawsuits over the next sixteen months. In February 1994, Carolco sued Viacom and Tri-Star to break the contracts they had signed with Golan. These companies, in turn, countersued and sued Marvel, too. Golan filed a lawsuit demanding that he be named as producer of any* Spider-Man *movie that should ever be made. MGM then filed suit, claiming it owned all* Spider-Man *rights. Finally, Marvel itself, which had sold the movie rights to* Spider-Man *three times in the thirteen years before this, now claimed that all those deals had expired and that all the movie rights had reverted to Marvel once more. As if this wasn't enough, during that period, 21st Century, Carolco, and Marvel all went into bankruptcy. Finally, to embellish this Keystone Kops situation, Marvel had also sold Golan the rights to* Captain America *in 1985, and the lawyers in the* Spider-Man *lawsuits kept confusing provisions of the* Captain America *contract with the* Spider-Man *contract. Losing important materials on their computers, the key parties ultimately were compelled to reconstruct evidence from memory.*

All the players had made a mess of the Spider-Man project. With all the countless still-pending lawsuits, the attorneys' fees were skyrocketing for everybody, including cash-strapped MGM. So, by 1999, most parties finally decided to settle. Compromises were made, the rights' issues were worked out, and, as MGM gave up all claims to Spider-Man, Columbia Pictures—a subsidiary of Sony—pledged to push ahead with the first Spider-Man feature movie.

Because of all the delays and confusion, I regretted that somewhere along the line we lost Jim Cameron as the writer/director of the film. I can imagine how bad he must have felt. The poor guy ended up doing *Titanic,* the biggest-grossing movie of all, which, I hope, assuaged his sorrow somewhat.

But just like all good comicbook stories, the *Spider-Man* movie saga has a happy ending. Marvel was lucky that one of our most talented young directors, Sam Raimi, had been a Spidey fan while growing up, and, you guessed it, even as I write these drama-drenched words, Sam is doing a sensational job of bringing the enthralling exploits of everybody's favorite friendly neighborhood web-slinger to the big screen. I had met Sam some years earlier when we were both planning to collaborate on a screenplay for *The Mighty Thor,* a collaboration that, like so many other of life's plans, never came to fruition. But I grew to know and become very fond of the only A-list director I know who unfailingly wears a shirt and tie, and often a suit jacket, while working on the set. He's young, conservatively dressed, soft-spoken, knows what he's doing, and easy to get along with. How did he ever make it in Hollywood?

Most important of all, I know Sam's the perfect guy to shepherd the Spidey movie, because he himself reminds me of a young Peter Parker.

Oh, I almost forgot to mention the most important thing of all. You know what'll really guarantee that *Spider-Man* will be a box-office bonanza? Yours truly can be spotted for a split-second in one of the scenes! I can just picture throngs of people flocking to theaters everywhere, as they incredulously ask each other, "You mean the guy is still around? I've gotta see that for myself!"

I'm sure people wonder why a big star like me would do a humble walk-on. After all, didn't I have a leading role in Kevin Smith's *Mallrats?* Wasn't I a featured player in Larry Cohen's *The Ambulance?* And is it mere coincidence that none of those films were box-office blockbusters? If anyone else wants to jinx a movie, call my agent. I'm available for a major role.

Although, come to think of it, I also appeared in *X-Men,* and that film was a smash hit. But that's probably because I was only on-screen for a couple of seconds, and positioned way in the background, with not a word to say. Bryan Singer, the director, sure knew what he was doing.

It would be unseemly to close this story without mentioning one almost unbelievable thing that happened to Stan, a thing that nobody ever expected to see. Even though his memory leaves a lot to be desired, this particular chapter in his extraordinary life happened recently enough that he probably remembers all of the surprising details vividly, and nobody can tell it better than the man himself.

It happened after I signed my new Marvel contract. The word got around that I was now free to accept any and all writing assignments—from anyone, anywhere.

One of the first people I heard from was Michael Uslan, a friend of mine who is one of the producers of the *Batman* movies. He came to see me and after the usual "How've you been?" repartee he cautiously broached a most unusual subject.

"Stan," said he, "how'd you like to write a series of comics for DC?"

Naturally I laughed. I've been associated with Marvel since

dinosaurs walked the earth. There's no way DC, our biggest competitor, would have me write for any of their mags.

Michael still looked serious. That started to worry me. I was aware that he's very closely connected with the DC hierarchy. He said he wasn't just talking about a few isolated stories. He wanted to know if I'd like to take DC's twelve most famous characters and write them as if I myself had created them. I'd be free to do them any way I wanted to.

Naturally, I told Michael (he doesn't answer to "Mike," no matter how long you've known him) that it was an assignment no writer in comics could ever turn down, but there was as much chance of DC letting me go wild with their top characters as there would be of Jay Leno taking over the David Letterman show and doing his Top Ten List. Michael got a sly look on his face and said, as he left, "No harm in my asking. I'll let you know."

I forgot all about it until a week later when Michael called and said, "You've got a deal!"

I suddenly realized I was committed. (And some might say I should have been.) That's when I started to worry. The series was to be called *Just Imagine If Stan Lee Created—* followed by the name of the superhero and the artist's name in each successive issue. The characters were to be Superman, Batman, Wonder Woman, the Flash, the Green Lantern, the Justice League, etc.—a dazzling dozen of DC's most important titles, each one to be drawn by a different top-name artist.

The reason I started to worry was, I know how long those characters have been around, how much their fans love them. What would the reaction be if I decided to make Batman a black guy from the 'hood, or Wonder Woman a Latina peasant girl who works for a Los Angeles magazine, or Aquaman a character who's actually made out of water? (And I did just that!) See what I mean? Would the rabid fans lynch me? Would people think I was off my rocker?

Well, to be honest, I only worried for about thirty seconds. It

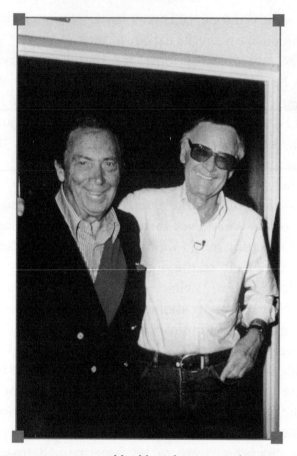

During a TV interview, my good buddy Bob Kane tried to mention Batman more times than I could mention Spider-Man. Guess who won?

was too challenging an assignment to turn down. So I went for it. And, y'know what? The books are doing great! And the fans haven't yet burned me in effigy—as far as I know.

But in case you're worried about how I'll keep busy when I've finished the last of the twelve-issue series for DC, there's something else going on in my life that might give me enough material for another bio-autography.

In fact, this may be my biggest thing yet . . .

Now, for My Next Number . . .

Genial George Mair, my capricious collaborator on this one-of-a-kind bio-autography, told me he thought that I should write the final chapter of this merrily meandering manuscript all by myself. He tried to make it sound like generosity on his part, but I suspect he simply found another victim for himself and is eager to get on to his next bio. Well, why not?

I'm beginning to realize it's an awesome responsibility having an entire chapter to oneself. But the toughest part is, how will I know where to end it? At what part of my life should I wrap it up? Since I'm still insanely involved with a whole kaboodle of projects, at what point should I write "The End"? A person's career isn't like a movie. As long as you're alive, there's no dramatic fade-out shot, accompanied by suitable music as the credits roll. And I'll be damned if I'll shrug off this mortal coil just to furnish you with a dramatic ending!

Of course, I could always just retire and that would give the book a nice, warm, uncomplicated ending. In fact, people are always asking when I plan to retire. I don't mind them asking, though I don't like it when their tone sounds hopeful. I always ask them, retire to what? Most people retire in order to finally do the things they really want to do. But I'm already doing them. I can't think of anything better than tackling new movie and TV projects with a bunch of talented, enthusiastic, creative people.

Chapter 21

Besides, when something's good, I hate to give it up. Maybe that's why I've had the same job at Marvel for more than half a century, the same wife for more than fifty years, the same accountant, Irwin Shapiro, for more than forty years, the same home for more than twenty, even the same housekeeper, the wonderful Alicia Ulloa, ever since we moved to L.A. Hell, even my favorite car is now fifteen years old! Come to think of it, if I didn't know me, I'd think I'm a real dull stick-in-the-mud. It's a good thing I know me.

So I guess all that remains is for me to tell you what I'm up to at present. But don't worry, when the last paragraph rolls around I'll try to think of some kind of dramatic finish. If you've hung with me this long I guess you deserve it.

One thing of monumental insignificance that I might mention is our menagerie. Joanie and I both love animals. At present we have three dogs and two cats, plus a family of six raccoons that come around every other night for their dinner. But the ironic part about it all is this—in the past, when we lived on Long Island, we always had big dogs. We had shepherds, Rottweilers, and Dobermans, not all at the same time, of course. We had given those great dogs great names, such as Simba, Growler, Tiger—you get the idea. Well, since I've allowed my wife to choose our pets, we now have two small Yorkies named Winky Dink and Pixie, plus a China Pug named Pookie. Can you imagine how I feel when Joanie says to me, "Stan, call the dogs in for dinner," and I have to bellow, "Here, Winky Dink! C'mon, Pixie. Where are you, Pookie?" Me, who's always been the essence of macho! Oh, how the mighty have fallen. We also have a feral cat who hates us. He comes around daily to be fed, snarling and spitting at us all the while. I named him Diablo. He's mean and angry. Him I love. And I almost forgot, my wife's cat's name is Eloise. Her I never call.

But, before I allow myself to wallow in a sea of self-pity, there's another odd thing I might mention. I seem to have become the uncrowned King of Introduction Writers. I can't even count how many times in the past dozen years people have asked me to write intros, prefaces, and forewords to their books. I'm talking comicbooks, pocketbooks, coffee table books, how-to books, whatever. You name any particular genre and the chances are I've written one or more intros for it.

Of course, that's just another example of my keen, razor-sharp business acumen. Introduction writers hardly ever receive royalties, no matter how well a book may sell. Yep, that's me, an acclaimed specialist in a virtually nonpaying field.

However, I persevere . . .

Having given up the late lamented Stan Lee Media, I turned to my dear friend and lawyer (always in that order!), the ever-amazing Arthur Lieberman, whose organizational wizardry and astonishing business acumen guided me in creating a new company called POW! Entertainment. The initials of POW! stand for "Purveyors of Wonder!" (Which I'm sure you've already guessed!) The exclamation point is there to remind me of my comicbook background.

My coconspirators and I will be creating and producing movies and TV series, both live and animated. At present, the entire company consists of he who is a shining shield 'gainst unseemly forms of villainy, the aforementioned Arthur Lieberman, our legal and business affairs maven as well as chief strategist and expert at Keeping Stan Out of Trouble; and my good friend and colleague, show-biz veteran, hands-on manager and simply superb team player, Gill Champion, who'll function as chief operating officer. Then there's mighty Mike Kelly, whose been my assistant for the past decade or so, who helps me with fan mail, handling the traffic on the *Spider-Man* strip, and just about anything else I toss at him; plus the ever-jubilant Junko Kobayashi, whose fantastic facility with facts and figures has earned her the coveted title of controller of POW!

That's them, our entire far-flung staff. As you can see, our little organization will be lean and mean—a far cry from SLM's more than 150 employees.

In the unpretentious yet dynamic offices of POW!, our highly

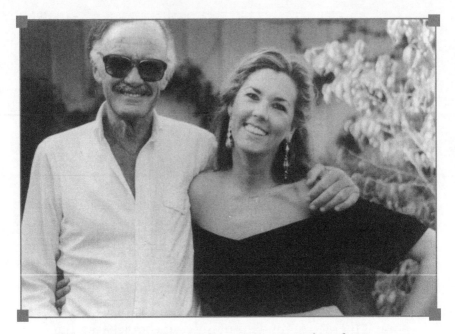

I'll bet you'd never suspect that Joanie was making faces at J.C. and me on the other side of the camera.

motivated, high-concept creative machine is presently developing projects on a first-look basis with Metro-Goldwyn-Mayer. Naturally, we're concentrating on motion pictures and TV, in both live-action and animation. In fact, we currently have one movie and two TV series in development, and are busily engaged in co-branding properties for all forms of the media.

Additionally, my novel, *The Alien Factor,* is under consideration for a major motion picture (no one ever seems to work on a "minor" motion picture!) and I'm starting to create new super-hero characters for an international sports and candy combine, besides planning new interactive games, CD-ROMs and projects which center around the exciting world of pop music.

As you've probably guessed, if any form of today's entertain-

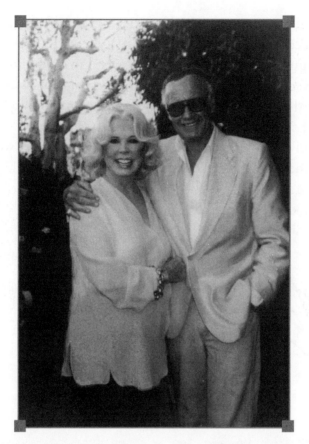

Comics, animation, show biz—maybe I did okay, maybe not.
But if she's still smiling after more than fifty years of marriage,
that's all that really matters!

ment can reach the public, there's no way that POW! and I won't be a part of it.

Besides my family, I guess the best thing about life today is that every time the phone rings, it has the potential to be someone offering an exciting new project for us, and every time I open a letter from some movie studio or TV network there's always the chance it'll mean a new film or series in the offing—and there's still the occasional comicbook that I'm asked to write.

So things are more exciting than ever. I'm doing just what I've always loved to do, creating characters and concepts with which to entertain the public, but now I'm doing it on the largest playing field of all.

It's all so different from the first time I started working in comics, when I figured I'd hang with it for a while until I got some experience and then I'd go out and get into the real world.

I think I just might be ready now.

Excelsior!

Photo Credits